PIONEER SETTLEMENT OF NEBRASKA TERRITORY

BASED ON THE ORIGINAL SURVEY
1855-66

Charles Howard Richardson, Ph.D.
University of Nebraska, 1968

Order this book online at www.trafford.com
or email orders@trafford.com

Most Trafford titles are also available at major online book retailers.

Printed in the United States of America.

ISBN: 978-1-4269-5717-8 (sc)
ISBN: 978-1-4269-5718-5 (e)

Trafford rev. 02/17/2011

 www.trafford.com

North America & international
toll-free: 1 888 232 4444 (USA & Canada)
phone: 250 383 6864 • fax: 812 355 4082

TABLE OF CONTENTS

ACKNOWLEDGMENT

The completion of a study of this kind necessarily involves the assistance and cooperation of several persons.

The writer gratefully acknowledges the valuable guidance and constructive criticism during all phases of the study given by his adviser and chairman of his committee, Dr. Leslie Hewes. Also, acknowledgment is due the other members of his committee: Dr. Charles B. McIntosh, Dr. Colbert C. Held, Dr. William W. Ray, Dr. Robert R. Dykstra, and Dr. J. A. Fagerstrom.

Thanks are extended to Mr. Willis L. Brown, State Surveyor, for providing access to the records of the original land survey and for his insight into the nature of them.

The encouragement and assistance of my wife, Norma H. Richardson, is also gratefully recognized.

INTRODUCTION

Major sources for determination and evaluation of the distribution of pioneer settlement in eastern Nebraska Territory included field books and township plats of the original land survey, 1855-1866, Territorial newspapers, and the census of 1860. Features of settlement and groves of timber existed in the area of study at the time of survey without having been mentioned in field notes or shown on plats. Section interiors on most occupied plats were under-represented with respect to fields, dispersed houses, and groves of timber. Yet, records of survey are believed to provide a representative sample of the distribution of pioneer features that existed during this early phase of settlement.

Survey records of public lands show that settlement was localized largely in the Missouri Valley, its larger tributary valleys, and the Platte Valley. Generally, settlement densities decreased upriver. Navigability of the Missouri River as well as presence of timber and water were major factors associated with distribution of early settlement. The Missouri was a busy route of steamboat traffic during the Territorial period; but inland rivers including the Platte were impassible. It seems that nowhere west of the Missouri River could merchandise from St. Louis be delivered so economically to equip emigrants and freighters. In the zone where major overland routes crossed the Missouri River, Nebraska City, Omaha City, and large towns became favored points for supplying freighters and outfitting emigrants who were headed for the West. Consequently, the Missouri Valley in Nebraska was more highly urbanized than most areas of early pioneering farther east. By comparison, the Platte Valley was less densely settled. The left bank of the Platte River was followed by an important overland wagon road. Here were a string of ranches and farmhouses. Troops from Fort Kearney protected settlers and emigrants from migratory bands of Indians who sometimes caused trouble along the western Platte Valley. Water and wood, especially cottonwood timber, were available along the Platte River. Probably, the Platte carried a perennial flow of water during the years of survey, at least as reported by surveyors.

Except along the Platte, Nebraska pioneers looked westward toward an unfamiliar environment, the open prairies of the outlying territory. Almost everywhere confronted by inadequate amounts of water and wood, pioneers had little success in settling there. Surveyors did not record any pioneers who ventured so far onto open prairies as to necessitate construction of sod houses. Few early settlers located more than ten miles from the Missouri and Platte valleys. Those who entered back country located along large tributaries where water and wood were relatively abundant. Generally, prairie farmers remained within sight of timber.

In settled areas near the border between prairie and forest, modes of occupance by pioneer farmers were aimed at ways of occupying small prairie uplands and, at the same time, utilizing wood. Commonly, early settlers located their claims so as to include both prairie and timber land, with about 20 acres of the latter. Some prairie farmers who held upland claims that were devoid of timber also claimed woodlots that were located in bottomland timber, several miles away. Other farmers who lived in river towns cultivated small fields of 10 or 20 acres on upland prairies. These fields were located along wagon roads near town. Because timber was in short supply, it was common for pioneers to fence small fields of cropland rather than to fence large pasturages needed for livestock. Also, a few farmers used sod to build their fences. Generally, livestock were left to roam at large.

Boundaries of the Area of Study

The eastern third of Nebraska Territory was chosen for study since it was surveyed during the earliest period of settlement prior to statehood, March 1, 1867, in the period between 1855 and 1866. The area of study is shaped like a flat topped pyramid, including about 24,000 square

CHAPTER II

NUCLEATED SETTLEMENT

Classification of Nucleated Settlements

Most occupied townsites that were recorded by the surveyors were surveyed, put on record in the County Recorder's Office, and settled, as shown by the dates of survey on plats having townsites, within the first five years of the Territorial period, 1854-1867. Thirty four nucleated settlements were recorded by 1858. Generally, townsites occupied from one fourth to one section of land. The most common size for townsites was one quarter section, but the largest, that of Omaha City, occupied three sections. In order to distinguish the similarities and differences among compact settlements, they have been classified into five sizes depending upon the number of houses in each, as shown in Table 3.

None of the compact settlements were estimated to have had more than 200 houses, and only two of them included more than 100 houses. A few large nucleated settlements had remarkable concentrations of houses. Two cities and five large towns included almost two thirds of the houses. The remaining one third of the houses was included within 27 small compact settlements, each having fewer than 50 houses.

TABLE 3

CLASSIFICATION OF NUCLEATED SETTLEMENTS

Class	Number of Settlements	Number of Houses	Per cent of Houses	Dates of Survey
Cities	2	100-200	32	1856
Large towns	5	50—99	31	1856
Small towns	7	25—49	20	1856-1858
Villages	8	10—24	12	1856-1858
Hamlets	12	2—9	5	1856-1857

Perhaps the most important insights to be gained about the settlement process are the early start of urbanization in the Territorial period and the rapidity of settlement differentiation into compact settlements of widely ranging sizes, in the short span of five years.

Distribution of Nucleated Settlements

Most early settlers of eastern Nebraska lived in compact settlements instead of rural localities. About 70 per cent of the pioneer houses recorded by the surveyors or estimated from other sources listed in Appendix A, were located at townsites, leaving only about 30 per cent of the dwellings dispersed within rural hinterlands (Table 5, p. 104). Including the 37 per cent of under-represented dispersed dwellings that are estimated to have been present, however, a more complete approximation of the rural proportion actually present is about 34 per cent. Accordingly, only about 66 per cent of the total houses are believed to have been located in nucleated settlements. Of the houses in compact settlements, more than two thirds were located in the southern part of the Missouri Valley, and about one fourth of them in the northern part, north of DeSoto. Less than one tenth of them were place din the eastern Platte Valley, east of Columbus.

The ratio of nucleated houses to dispersed dwellings varied from region to region. For example, the north Missouri Valley was the most highly nucleated. Here, about 87 per cent of the houses were located at townsites (Table 5). However, considering the under-representation of dispersed dwellings by the surveyors, about 83 per cent is a more complete estimate of the proportion of houses that occupied compact settlements. In the south Missouri Valley, about 75 per cent of the houses were built in townsites. With the qualification of under-representation in mind, about 57 per cent is a more complete estimate of the proportion of houses actually in nucleated settlements. The east Platte Valley was least nucleated of the areas having some concentration of nucleated settlement. Here, only 50 per cent of the houses were located in compact settlements. Again, based on the under-representation of dispersed dwellings, about 44 per cent is a more complete estimate of the proposition of dwellings that were actually nucleated there. The country west of the major river valleys, the outlying territory, had no compact settlements except the hamlet with only two dwellings, namely Saltville.

In the south Missouri Valley, about 90 per cent of its nucleated houses were included within compact settlements that have been classified for this study as cities and large towns (Table 4). The south Missouri Region was estimated to have had about 760 houses that were located in 17 townsites. Its full complement of urban classes included two cities, five large towns, one small town, one village, and eight hamlets. The cities included about 45 per cent of the nucleated houses, and large towns had about the same proportion.

TABLE 4

REGIONAL TABULATION OF NUCLEATED SETTLEMENT[1]

	Regions of Settlement				
	Eastern Nebraska Territory	South Missouri Valley	North Missouri Valley	East Platte Valley	Outlying Territory
Numbers of:					
Cities	2	2	0	0	0
Large towns	5	5	0	0	0
Small towns	7	1	5	1	0
Villages	8	1	5	2	0
Hamlets	12	8	2	1	1
Total	34	17	12	4	1
Platted townsites	22	14	4	4	4
Houses in:					
Cities	350	350	0	0	0
Large towns	340	340	0	0	0
Small towns	237	25	172	40	0
Villages	133	11	86	36	0
Hamlets	55	35	14	4	2
Total	1115	761	272	80	2
Per cent of nucleated houses in:					
Cities	31	46	0	0	0
Large towns	31	45	0	0	0
Small towns	21	3	63	50	0
Villages	12	1	32	45	0
Hamlets	5	5	5	5	100

1   Table 4 includes house counts from the records of the original land survey, a few territorial newspapers and estimates from the 1860 census of population. Page 79 states the qualifications that apply to these tabulations.

TABLE 5

REGIONAL MEASURES OF NUCLEATED SETTLEMENT

Areas of Settlement	Total Nucleated Settlement	Total Nucleated Houses	Per cent of Nucleated Houses[2]	Per cent Urban[3]	Nucleated Density per Settled Township[4]
South Missouri	17	761	69	75	15
North Missouri	12	272	24	87	12
East Platte	4	80	7	50	5
West Platte	0	0	0	0	0
Outlying territory	1	2	0	7	0
Eastern Nebraska	34	1116	100	70	10

The small towns included only about three per cent of the agglomerated houses. Although most numerous, hamlets had only about five per cent of the nucleated dwellings. The single village of this region had only about one per cent of the agglomerated houses. Here, dispersed houses were especially abundant, more so than in any other region.

The north Missouri Valley, lacking cities and large towns, had about 95 per cent of its agglomerated houses concentrated in small towns and villages. This region held an estimated 270 houses in twelve townsites: five small towns, five villages, and two hamlets. Small towns included 64 per cent of the nucleated houses; villages had almost one third of them. Only about five per cent of the agglomerated houses were in hamlets. Here, the count of dispersed houses from the records of the original land survey was especially low.

In the east Platte Valley, about one half of the nucleated houses were incorporated in villages and hamlets. This region, which also

2   The proportion of all houses in nucleated settlements of eastern Nebraska computed for each area of settlement.

3   The ratio of the number of the houses in nucleated settlements to the total number of dwellings within each area of settlement.

4   Equals the number of houses at nucleated settlements within each area of settlement divided by the number of townships that were settled there.z

included Fontenelle in the Elkhorn Valley, had an estimated 80 houses in four townsites. There were located in this region: one small town, two villages, and one hamlet. Small towns had about one half of the agglomerated houses, and villages contained about 45 per cent of them. Only five per cent of the nucleated houses were estimated to have been included in hamlets. On the other hand, dispersed houses were relatively abundant here, considerably more so than along the northern Missouri Valley.

Characteristics of Nucleated Settlements

In this section, nucleated settlements are characterized according to the following sequence of classes: cities, large towns, small towns, villages, and hamlets. The direction that pioneering took and the spatial arrangement of early settlements govern the order of presentation. Within individual classes, consequently, agglomerated settlements are listed in the order that they appeared to the pioneers as they headed upstream along the length of the valley systems, first the Missouri and then the Platte. Particular attention is directed toward the natural resources near townsites, to the kind and variety of transportational links to each townsite, and to the role played by each compact settlement in the pioneer economy. Platted townsites, or paper towns, are discussed generally as to their role in the pioneering process.

Cities. During 1856, Nebraska City, "about 150 houses" with the large towns of South Nebraska City "about 50 houses" and Kearney City "about 75 houses", if counted as a unit, comprised the largest urban agglomeration in the Territory.[5] The sites of these three nucleated settlements occupied about one section of hilly prairie adjacent to the channel of the Missouri River (Figure 6). Although the surrounding land was rated by the surveyors as "good quality" for cultivation, it was sparsely settled possibly because there was not enough lumber in the few scattered "groves of oak and hickory"[6] for the construction of farmhouses. Although local timber was in short supply, these three townsites offered the advantage of a channelside position where a good

---

5 U.S.L.S., Nebraska Territory, *Field Notes*, T8N, R14E, January 1-29, 1856.

6 *Ibid.*

steamboat landing was convenient and where a heavily traveled ferry served the city. Kearney City had "an old and well established ferry".[7] Soon after 1857, this crossing received a new steam ferryboat (Figure 4). Further evidences of the transportational importance of Nebraska City were the stagecoach lines that reached to all parts of the Territory. The stage office was located within a two-story hotel that was built in 1854.[8] Nearby, a large barn was equipped to care for the numerous horses owned by the stagecoach companies.

Located almost due east of Fort Kearney, the urban agglomerations of Nebraska City, South Nebraska City, and Kearney City, had an advantageous situation that enabled them to grow in size and commercial importance. Nebraska City became a preferred site, on a direct route between the Missouri River and Fort Kearney, for the bulk breaking of river freight, for the outfitting of emigrants, and for the organization of wagon trains. The golden days of Nebraska City existed during 1858, when Russell, Majors, and Waddell selected it as the starting point for freight transactions to the West.[9] The variety of warehouses, stores, and manufacturing shops offered not only many job opportunities for the settlers but also a wide selection of goods and services for the emigrants. Even during the panic of 1857, Nebraska City remained in the best financial condition of any city in Nebraska because it had the only bank that remained solvent.[10] During the panic, the city continued to expand. It was reported that, "a block of fine buildings in our city is nearly completed by the Nebraska City Building Company. In it are commodious store rooms, and halls for various purposes, and also small rooms suitable for offices."[11]

In 1856, Omaha City had, according to an estimate, about 1200 inhabitants and 200 houses.[12] At this time, it was expanded by the Pierce and Omaha City Company additions to include 3 sections of land.[13]

---

7   *Nebraska News*, January 17, 1857.
8   Andreas, A. T. *History of the State of Nebraska*, Chicago: The Western Historical Company, 1882, p. 1201.
9   *Ibid.*, p. 1203.
10 *Nebraska News*, December 19, 1857, p. 2.
11 *Nebraska News*, January 17, 1857.
12 Estimate is based upon the 1860 census of population for Nebraska Territory.
13 U.S.L.S., *op. cit., Plat*, T15N, R13E, June 10-14, 1856.

The city encompassed mostly rolling prairie adjacent to the Missouri River channel. Beyond the city, the township included bottomland with a "sandy loam soil that was sometimes subject to overflow."[14] The remainder of the township was "second rate, high rolling prairie with clay loam soil."[15] Although timber was scarce, there were "groves of oak, ash, elm, walnut, and hickory," that occupied the eastern tier of section, and the bottomland was partially timbered with cottonwood.[16] There was sufficient local timber to support the construction of a few farm houses, but small fields were far more numerous than farm houses, particularly along wagon roads leading from the city.

Omaha City, like Nebraska City, was a major site for emigrant outfitting. Omaha City was linked directly by wagon road to Fort Kearney via the left bank of the Platte River. In 1856, it was claimed that steamboats unloaded pioneers and freight each day during the season of navigation.[17] Moreover, streams of emigrants and their wagon trains crossed the Missouri River here at the steam ferry crossing. Prior to the technological advances in transportation and communication that were so advantageous to its growth, Omaha City was already a bustling commercial center. The variety of stores and manufacturing shops that offered job opportunities for the settlers and provisions for the emigrants included a bank, food and clothing stores, a hotel, the Hamilton House, and a blacksmith shop.[18] The diversity of goods and services here made it the most attractive outfitting center for emigrants north of the Platte.

In the latter half of the Territorial period, technological advances, especially in communication and transportation, were important to the continuous rise of Omaha City from a pristine townsite with one log house in January, 1855, to the preeminent city of the Territory. Attracted to this city because it had been chosen previously as the Territorial capital, the Pacific Telegraph Company located its main headquarters here.[19] This decision, it was claimed, foretold the choice of Omaha City as the main office for the Union Pacific Railroad Company. The

14 U.S.L.S., *op. cit., Field Notes*, T16N, R13E, May 29-June 9, 1856.
15 *Ibid.*
16 *Ibid.*
17 *The Nebraskian*, June 25, 1856.
18 *Nebraska News*, December 19, 1857.
19 *Huntsman's Echo*, July 26, 1860.

decision to begin construction of this railroad in 1863 from Omaha City through the Platte Valley proved to be the keystone for the long-term, accelerated growth of this city. This forecast was made as early as March, 1856:

> Fourteen months ago Omaha City was almost a wilderness with only one log house decorating its surface. Now Omaha is a rising and successful western city – the emporium of the West – the depot of the immense trade between the Atlantic and the Pacific. A great line of railroads – the greatest in the world – from New York to Chicago by the foot of the lakes passes through us, and thence via Fontenelle and Buchanan to the shores of the Pacific. Contracts are already being closed for the actual completion of the great iron highway. Nothing can prevent Omaha City from becoming one of the greatest cities of the West, not excepting Chicago and St. Louis.[20]

Large Towns. In 1856, Plattsmouth was estimated to have included about 50 houses.[21] This large town was a major site of emigrant outfitting and debarkation leading from the Missouri River. Located on the rolling uplands beside the Missouri River and south of the Platte, it had a good steamboat landing and a heavily traveled ferry across the Missouri River. Emigrants embarked from here toward Fort Kearney along a cutoff route or along the route leading to the right bank of the Platte River. A variety of stores and manufacturing establishments indicated that this settlement was a busy market place for settlers and emigrants. Commercial establishments included a drug store, a general store, and a hotel, the Nebraska House.[22] Manufacturing establishments included two saw mills and a grist mill that produced livestock feed and 25 barrels of flour per day.[23] Besides the business generated by emigrants, farmers of the surrounding countryside marketed their agricultural commodities in this large town.[24] Some other advantages of Plattsmouth for settlement were the presence of the courthouse of Cass

20   *The Nebraskian*, March 19, 1856.
21   Estimate was derived from the 1860 census of territorial population.
22   Andreas, *op. cit.,* p. 482.
23   *Ibid.*, p. 483.
24   *Nebraska Advertiser*, June 7, 1856.

County and the anticipation of receiving the terminal of the Burlington and Missouri Railroad.[25] The township included timber and limestone. Groves of hardwoods occupied the uplands and good cottonwood grew on the bottoms.[26] From limestone outcroppings within the ravines, excellent limestone was quarried, according to the surveyors.

From infancy in 1856 when Bellevue was subdivided into lots, it grew rapidly to a large town estimated, on the basis of the 1860 census of population, to have included 90 houses in 1857. Located about one mile upstream from the mouth of Papillion Creek, Bellevue was a place of considerable importance for the outfitting of emigrants who headed directly along the wagon road toward the left bank of the Platte River. It had a good steamboat landing because Papillion Creek for a half mile in front of this large town, had a 10 to 15 foot limestone bank. Another asset of Bellevue was a well traveled boat service that ferried emigrants across the Missouri River to Bellevue. By 1857, it had a variety of commercial establishments that included four stores, the Fontenelle Bank of Bellevue, and two large hotels, the Benton House and Mission House.[27] It was the seat of Sarpy County, where a meeting was held to plan the building of the courthouse in 1857. In addition to the function of emigrant outfitting, Bellevue was an important market place for farmers of the densely settled Papillion Valley.[28]

Formerly called "Winter Quarters", Florence had "80 substantial buildings" in 1856.[29] This large town grew rapidly because it was an important overwintering place and rendezvous point for Mormons who wee headed for Salt Lake City.[30] It was the northernmost town along the Missouri Valley where emigrants could embark on a direct route to Fort Kearney by wagon road. The townsite occupied one section of land that provided a good steamboat landing because here the channel impinged against the river bluffs. Also, Florence had a steam ferryboat that carried heavy emigrant traffic across the Missouri River.[31] This relatively large settlement was thriving in 1856. The nature of its commercial and

25 *Nebraska Advertiser*, November 22, 1856.
26 U.S.L.S. *op. cit.*, T12N, R14E, May 9-12, 1856.
27 *Bellevue Gazette*, October 23, 1856.
28 *Ibid.*
29 *Nebraska Advertiser*, October 18, 1856.
30 *The Nebraskian*, July 23, 1856.
31 *Ibid.*

manufacturing establishments indicate that emigrant outfitting was an important function. A bank was near completion, and there were two large stores and a hotel. Also a site was purchased to erect an iron foundry, and saw mills as well as brick yards were in operation. During the early years of the Territorial period, Florence attracted not only emigrants but also settlers, and in 1856, all of the land in the township was claimed and much of it was improved.

Like so many other towns along the Missouri River, the future growth of Florence depended upon its ability to attract the Union Pacific Railroad. Its site and situation were advantageous for the terminal of this railroad, and to enhance its chances of attracting it, another large hotel was being planned in 1856.[32] Yet, Florence could not compete with Omaha City primarily because the latter's function as the Territorial capital was a stronger magnet than any advantage that Florence could offer to the Union Pacific Railroad.

Small Towns. In June, 1856, Brownville "contained about 24 houses".[33] At that time, this small town was growing rapidly in local trade and secondarily, in emigrant outfitting. Neighboring farmers marketed agricultural commodities there.[34] The variety of stores and manufacturing shops indicated that Brownville was a busy market place for settlers, transients, and some emigrants who were headed to the West. Commercial establishments included a hotel, general store, a dry goods shop, and a grocery.[35] Among the manufacturing shops were a cabinet shop, a blacksmith shop, a steam saw mill, and a brick manufactory.[36] Other features included churches, a school, and the courthouse of Nemaha County. When observed at the time of survey, the houses in Brownville gave the appearance of poor construction because they were built so hastily. The rapid settlement of Brownville was brought about by its favorable location. It was placed on 480 acres of rolling land beside the channel of the Missouri River, midway between Nebraska City and the southeast corner of the Territory. Here, it had a good steamboat landing, and it was served by a heavily traveled ferry.[37] Brownville was

32 *Nebraska Advertiser*, October 18, 1856.
33 U.S.L.S., *op. cit.*, T5N, R16E, January 24-31, 1856.
34 *Nebraska Advertiser*, June 7, 1856.
35 *Ibid.*
36 *Ibid.*
37 U.S.L.S., *op. cit.*

situated favorably with respect to the intervening destination of most emigrants, Fort Kearney. Yet, the surveyors indicated on their plats that no wagon road led directly along a cutoff route from Brownville to Fort Kearney. This fact, together with the relatively small size of Brownville, at the time of survey, suggest that here emigrant outfitting had a subordinate function compared to its predominant role at large settlements between Florence and Nebraska City.

Tekama was located in section 19 of T21N, R11E, partly on terrace land and partly on bluffs along the northern Missouri Valley. Being located about 5 miles from the river channel, it had neither a ferry crossing nor a steamboat landing. Instead, it was linked to the wagon road that paralleled the Missouri Valley. Tekama was settled by 24 pioneers of the Quincy Company in 1855,[38] and by late 1857, it had grown to a small town with "30 dwellings".[39] Although it did not have a hotel, this small town had an unusual feature that helped to explain its size. It was the penitentiary of the Nebraska Territory.[40] Other features that helped to sustain it were the seat of Burt County, a story, and a blacksmith shop.[41] Furthermore, two steam saw mills operated within 800 acres of cottonwood timber near the Missouri River.

The fate of Omadi, located in T27N, R9E, was the same as that of many early towns that were placed in the Missouri Valley. By 1858, the west bank of the channel began to erode, and by 1865 all the buildings of Omadi had eroded away.[42] Located on dry benchland on the banks of the Missouri near the mouth of Omaha Creek, in 1860, this small town had "40 houses, all nice frame ones".[43] Although Omadi was never abandoned until it was physically destroyed, "some houses were left unoccupied when the owners rushed to Pike's Peak" in the spring of 1859.[44] Certainly, this rapid exodus of pioneers from Omadi indicates the mobile nature of early settlement in eastern Nebraska. To accommodate the traveling public along the Missouri River, Omadi had a hotel, called the American House. Other indicators of its once

---

38   Andreas, *op. cit.,* p. 402.

39   U.S.L.S., *op. cit.* T21N, R11E, November 27-December 3, 1857.

40   *Ibid.*

41   Andreas, *op. cit.,* page 420.

42   *Ibid.,* p. 610.

43   *Dakota City Herald*, February 4, 1860.

44   *Ibid.*

flourishing appearance were a store, a warehouse, a school, and two steam saw mills.[45] In 1858, Dakota was the fastest growing settlement of the northern Missouri Valley. Although a small town of "25 or 30 houses" at the time of survey,[46] it expanded to "65 or 70 houses" by November 1859.[47] Dakota had the northernmost ferry crossing of the Missouri River (Figure 4), and despite its floodplain site, the steamboat landing was excellent. This ferry received heavy use from the emigrants who crossed the Missouri River here while en route to the Platte Valley. Noteworthy of a small town, Dakota was an outfitting center for emigrants, although less important than the primary centers between Florence and Nebraska City. The variety of stores and manufacturing shops indicated its capacity to provide the goods and services needed by the emigrants. There was a dry goods store, a grocery store, a blacksmith shop, and some saddle shops, and some law offices.[48] Dakota met the needs of the traveling public with two hotels. The Bates House was a three-story hotel with a two-story wing,[49] and, the Chihuahua House had been remodeled from a log cabin that had a sod roof and a dirt floor. Other functions of this small town added to its importance. It was the seat of Dakota County and it held the United States Land Office. Its pottery was said to be the most extensive stoneware manufactory on the Missouri River. It shipped out 8,000 to10,000 pieces of earthenware during October, 1859. In a few years Dakota was expected to receive yet another stimulus for its growth, the terminal of the Dubuque and Pacific Railroad.

Logan had a short disastrous history. In 1858, "it contained 30 houses beside the bank of the Missouri River."[50] At that time, it was not much smaller than other towns within the northern Missouri Valley. However, by 1860, Logan had been deserted. The abandonment of Logan can be attributed to several factors. The first of these was its disadvantageous position with respect to Dakota, located beside the channel of the Missouri River. Logan was slightly off the emigrant route that crossed the Missouri River at Dakota and then turned southward

45 *Ibid.*
46 U.S.L.S., *op. cit.*, T28N, R9E, March 10-13, 1858.
47 *Dakota City Herald*, November 26, 1859.
48 *Dakota City Herald*, November 26, 1859.
49 *Dakota City Herald*, August 13, 1859.
50 U.S.L.S., *op. cit.*

toward the Platte Valley. Like most small towns, it had a hotel that accommodated the traveling public along the Missouri Valley. Secondly, fire contributed to its decline. A prairie fire engulfed Logan on October 22, 1856, when a house, a storeroom, some lumber, and 100 tons of hay wee burned.[51] In the vicinity of Logan, there was neither very much rural settlement nor timber. However, one mile from Logan, a saw mill was located within a grove called "Logan Timber". The scarcity of timber in this area may have been a circumstance that explains why a strong wind swept the prairie fire into this settlement.

St. Johns was a small Irish town whose pioneers came there from Dubuque, Iowa. In 1857 "it contained 200 voters"[52] but the 1860 census of population records only 44 people. Considering the rapid decline in population between 1857 and 1860, it is difficult to estimate the number of houses at the time of survey, 1858. Perhaps 45 houses is a reasonable estimate, but there may have been more considering the small percentage of women in the population and the youthfulness of the settlers. It was located nine miles northwest of Dakota among the scenic bluffs of the Missouri River. It had no ferry crossing but it was linked by access road to the wagon road that paralleled the Missouri Valley. Unlike most small towns of eastern Nebraska, St. Johns did not have a hotel to accommodate the traveling public. Yet, it did have a store and manufacturing establishments that utilized the local natural resources. These were a steam saw mill, a shingle sawing machine, and a grist mill. In 1857, the well established character of this settlement was revealed by the Catholic Church and log school house.[53]

In December, 1855, the surveyor described Fontenelle as follows:

> The town of Fontenelle was laid out some two years since by the Fontenelle Company on an elevated part of ground a half-mile southwest of the Elkhorn River. It contains about 40 dwelling houses and has a fine steam saw mill in progress of erection. The town has every appearance of thrift and prosperity.[54]

51 *The Nebraskian*, October 22, 1856.
52 *Bellevue Gazette*, December 3, 1857.
53 Andreas, *op. cit.*, p. 613.
54 U.S.L.S., *op. cit.*, T18N, R9E, November 28-December 7, 1855.

During 1856, the prosperity of the small town of Fontenelle was evidenced by a store, and a hotel, the Fontenelle House.[55] This hotel housed some travelers from Florence who were headed either West along the Platte Valley or northwest along the Elkhorn Valley. The store gained some of its trade from farmers who lived west of Fontenelle on the wagon road along Maple Creek, a confluent of the Elkhorn River. Further evidence of Fontenelle's early importance was its role as the county seat of Dodge County until 1860, and as the site of a chartered college, the "Nebraska University".[56] However, the prosperity of this community declined during the latter part of the Territorial period primarily because the route chosen by the Union Pacific Railroad Company from Omaha City through the Platte Valley bypassed Fontenelle. Consequently, it could not market the agricultural commodities from its hinterland as rapidly as could Fremont, for instance, located on the Union Pacific Railroad.

Villages. In 1856, DeSoto comprised "10 or 12 houses and 20-25 inhabitants."[57] Here, the construction of buildings was easy because there were abundant stands of oak, and linden on the uplands and a scattering of cottonwood groves on the bottomland. It had two saw mills, one powered by steam and another by water.[58] Located about 25 miles north of Omaha City, DeSoto was about one-fourth mile south of the Missouri River. At the channel, it had a good steamboat landing and a busy ferry. In September, 1857, it was reported that, "the Desoto ferry was a frequent transit of teams, travelers, and peddlers across the Missouri River."[59] To serve the travelers along the Missouri Valley, this village had a hotel as early as 1856.[60] Other establishments included two stores, a wagon-makers shop, and a blacksmith shop. By having good wagon roads to inland settlements, some river towns gained the advantage of increased commerce. A critical hindrance to the growth of DeSoto stemmed from the lack of a wagon road to Fontenelle, a small town to the west of DeSoto. In 1856, farmers near Fontenelle could not

55 Andreas, *op. cit.*, pp. 1470-1471.
56 *Ibid.*,
57 U.S.L.S., *op. cit.*, T18N, R12E, March 16-26, 1856.
58 *The Nebraskian*, July 23, 1856.
59 *DeSoto Pilot*, September 19, 1857.
60 *he Nebraskian*, July 23, 1856.

market their produce in DeSoto.[61] Nor did DeSoto have a wagon road to Elkhorn. Even by 1856, the creeks were not bridged on the wagon road between DeSoto and Omaha City.

The surveyor had this to say about Cuming in March, 1856, "Cuming City is located in Section 34 [T19N, R11E] on a beautiful townsite on high level bench land. It is a new settlement but 12 months old containing 16 houses, and it has the appearance of thrift and prosperity".[62] One of the principal assets of Cuming was the ferry that served this crossing of the Missouri River.[63] North of this village, there was only one ferry, and it at Dakota. Moreover, it had a good landing for steamboats and a hotel was being built to accommodate the travelers along the Missouri Valley.[64] Besides the construction of a hotel, Cuming attempted to attract new settlers in two other ways. First, it acquired a charter for a new college named Washington College. Since the pioneers had considerable interest in higher education, this charter promised a popular cultural attraction for Cuming.[65] Secondly, four lots and enough timber to build a dwelling house were offered to each newcomer to Cuming who would erect his own house.[66] To facilitate construction, the community was in the process of erecting a new steam saw mill. Although scarce, there was some timber along North Heart Creek.

Harney was laid out directly across the Missouri River from the Iowa town of Sioux City. The surveyor had little to say about this settlement except: "on section 16 and a portion of section 17, the town of Harney City is laid off on which there are some 20 houses and 75 to 100 inhabitants".[67] It was located entirely on level floodplain. Part of this township was low and wet, and it was covered with willows. Along the bank of the Missouri River, there was cottonwood timber, and elsewhere the township was covered with prairie.[68] Although Harney was located close to several platted townsites, there were only a few farmsteads. It

---

61 *Ibid.,*

62 U.S.L.S., *op. cit.,* T19N, R11E, March 19-27, 1856.

63 *The Nebraskian,* April 2, 1856.

64 *Ibid.*

65 *Ibid.*

66 *Ibid.*

67 U.S.L.S., *op. cit.,* T29N, R9E, April 15-18, 1858.

68 *Ibid.*

seems likely that the poor drainage and lack of timber of this township may have hindered its settlement.

Ponca was described by the surveyor in 1858 as "a thriving little village containing a store, a blacksmith shop, a hotel, and several other buildings".[69] By 1860, it included "12 dwellings houses and two hotels: the Barrett's House and the Ponca House."[70] As evidence of its vitality, Ponca was the seat of Dixon County. Located about 25 miles northwest of Dakota, Ponca was placed two miles up Aowa Creek from the Missouri River. Therefore, it had neither a steamboat landing nor a ferry crossing. Yet, in 1860 the number of travelers along the wagon road that led to Ponca were numerous enough to support two hotels. Along Aowa Creek, there was timber suitable for house building. In 1858, the surveyor said, "There was sufficient timber adjoining the river to supply the demand on the prairie".[71]

In 1858, St. James was "a thriving village containing about 25 buildings". The business district included "a hotel, two stores, and a mechanics shop,"[72] and the courthouse of Cedar County was located here. This village was laid out at the mouth of Bow Creek where the Missouri River, its confluent, bordered South Dakota. This township was said to have, "the best land on the Missouri River above Sioux City, and contains some handsome farms; and it is tolerably well settled."[73] Although mostly high rolling prairie, it included a little bottomland along Bow Creek where the farmhouses were located. One mile east of the village, a saw mill was in operation. Here, the bluffs of the Missouri Valley were dotted with cedar. Along Bow Valley, there were many beaver workings near scattered groves of timber.

The "old cabin" of Niobrara was erected in 1856 for protection from the Ponca Indians who lived in a village west of the Niobrara River. During the winter of 1856-57, the Poncas burned all the houses of Niobrara except the old cabin, which by the report had logs 3 feet in diameter. Building materials were brought here on the steamer,

---

69 U.S.L.S., *op. cit.*, T30N, R6E, April 21-28, 1858.
70 *Dakota City Herald*, January 7, 1860.
71 U.S.L.S., *op. cit.*
72 U.S.L.S., *op. cit.*, T32N, R2E, November 10-15, 1858.
73 *Ibid.*

Omaha, in the summer of 1857 in order to rebuild the village.[74] In March, 1858, the surveyor said that Niobrara had "15 or 20 houses, a large and commodious hotel, and a saw mill."[75] This hotel housed those travelers who usually reached this settlement either by Missouri River steamboat or by stagecoach. Although Niobrara had no ferry crossing, the landing was accessible for steamboats at all times during the season of navigation. To supply their saw mill, the residents of this village depended upon "the valuable stands of timber" that grew on islands of the Niobrara River.[76]

Fremont functioned mainly as a market place for rural settlers and as a refitting stop for emigrants along the Platte Valley. It was laid out along the route of the Platte a few miles west of where this wagon road crossed the Elkhorn River. Therefore, emigrants who may have forgotten supplies or who needed emergency repairs could obtain them here. In 1857, Fremont comprised a "store, a post office, and 16 houses with others in the process of construction".[77] It may be assumed that this store traded with the pioneers of more than 15 farmhouses distributed along the route of the Platte. Here, the pioneers cultivated their fields on rich benchland that extended as far as one mile north of the Platte River. Furthermore, along Rawhide Creek, a small confluent of the Platte, the settlers found the soil especially black and rich.

Columbus claimed to be *the* pioneer village of Nebraska Territory at the time of original survey because it was placed farther west in the Platte Valley than any other settlement of its size.[78] It "contained about 20 houses and 10 or 15 families in 1858".[79] A saw mill, a grist mill, and a shingle mill operated here although timber was a scarce commodity. Only a few cottonwood were scattered along the river banks. The rapid growth of Columbus stemmed from its position at the ferry crossing of the Loup Fork River. Like other settlements on the emigrant route of the Platte, Columbus functioned not only as a market place for the surrounding farmers who cultivated the rich benchland but also

---

74 Andreas, *op. cit.*, pp. 1029-1030.
75 U.S.L.S., *op. cit.*, T32N, R6W, March 15-20, 1859.
76 *Ibid.*
77 U.S.L.S., *op. cit.*, T17N, R8E, September 8-24, 1857.
78 *The Nebraskian*, September 10, 1856.
79 U.S.L.S., *op. cit.*, T17N, R1E, October 15-20, 1858.

as a refitting stop for emigrants headed toward Fort Kearney. This important village included a tavern, a store, and several other buildings that were under construction.[80]

Hamlets. In 1863, when the Sac and Fox Reservation was surveyed, the surveyor said this about Falls City, "Falls City is a flourishing town of about 500 inhabitants in the north part of the township and has the appearance of thrift and prosperity".[81] The surveyor did not mention Falls City in the field notes of the original survey, 1856. At the time of survey, 1856, nine farmhouses were distributed along the Big Nemaha and Walnut floodplains. Primarily, Falls City depended upon trade with these farmers and those that settled later in its hinterland for its growth and sustenance. Farming was attractive in the locality of Falls City because the Big Nemaha and Walnut valleys had a considerable quantity of "fine quality soil".[82] There were other valuable resources including timber of good quality, mill sites, and a coal seam on Pony Creek.[83] Important for its long term growth, the courthouse and seat of Richardson County became situated permanently at Falls City.

Placed at the junction of the Big and Little Nemaha rivers, Salem was an agriculturally oriented hamlet. In February, 1856, the surveyor described it as follows: "The town of Salem is laid out on the south half of Section 3 on the southern slope of the bluff and near the forks of the river. It contains a saw mill, tavern, store, post office, and 3 dwelling houses."[84] The site of this hamlet was chosen at a central position among the 13 farmhouses of its township and near others in the locality. The surveyor said there was a considerable amount of timber along the Big Nemaha River, and the bottom of the Nemaha River was described as "rich and nearly all susceptible of cultivation".[85] By 1857, Salem had acquired some features that revealed its importance as an agricultural community. They included a courthouse, post office, blacksmith shop, and a plough factory.[86]

---

80 *Ibid.*
81 U.S.L.S., *op. cit.*, T1N, R16E, July 27, 1863.
82 *Ibid.*
83 *Ibid.*
84 U.S.L.S., *op. cit.*, T1N, R15E, November 15, 1855-February 6, 1856.
85 *Ibid.*
86 *Nebraska Advertiser*, April 16, 1857.

Bordering the western edge of the Half-Breed Tract, Archer was the trade center for nearly a dozen farmhouses that were distributed along Muddy Creek. In December, 1855, "Archer contained 5 houses and it was the seat of Richardson County".[87] Where the farmhouses were located, Muddy Creek had rich bottomland, and the flood plain had scattered groves of timber. The natural advantages of Archer's site are apparent, but proximity to the Half-Breed Reservation retarded its growth chiefly because the land in this tract was withdrawn from the public domain, from pioneer settlement, and from Archer's trade area. Consequently, in 1857, the county seat was transferred from here to Salem. Later, Falls City became the permanent seat of this county.

St. Deroin was located at the eastern margin of the Half-Breed Tract about 8 miles south of Nemaha. Facing the Missouri River from a bluff, it had a ferry crossing and a good landing. In 1856, this hamlet "contained 5 dwelling houses and a store".[88] Located within the Half-Breed Tract, it traded primarily with the half-blooded Indians who lived on farmsteads within this reservation. Seven farmhouses that belonged to the half-breeds were clustered nearby. In addition to the agricultural resources of this township, limestone, sandstone, and coal outcropped at several places within the ravines of the Missouri Valley. Moreover, the bluffs were timbered heavily with elm, oak, hickory, and walnut.[89]

Located at the mouth of the Little Nemaha River, Nemaha, like most hamlets, functioned primarily as a market place for neighboring farmers. A cluster of 6 farmhouses surrounded this hamlet, and others were placed close by on the flood plain of the Little Nemaha River. In describing Nemaha during 1856, the surveyors aid, "Nemaha City contains two dwelling houses and a store. It has a beautiful situation on a bluff 50 feet above the Missouri River bottomlands, having a gentle slope (ascent) to the north and west".[90] Nemaha had a ferry crossing of the Missouri River and a good steamboat landing at the river's edge. In order to attract newcomers and to encourage its rapid growth, the promoters of this hamlet offered to donate 100 lots to each pioneer who would actually settle here.[91]

87 U.S.L.S., *op. cit.*, T2N, R16E, November 21-December 5, 1855.
88 U.S.L.S., *op. cit.*, T4N, R16E, July 29-August 7, 1856.
89 *Ibid.*
90 U.S.L.S., *op. cit.*, T4N, R15E, August 25-30, 1856.
91 *Nebraska Advertiser*, August 30, 1856.

Kanoshe was located 3 miles south of Rock Bluffs on the wagon road that linked Plattsmouth with Nebraska City. In the general description of the township during 1856, the surveyor described these hamlets as follows:

> There are 2 towns laid out, recorded, and incorporated in this township. The town of Kanoshe is in fractional section 33, and has 8 or 9 buildings and 6 or 7 families. The town of Rock Bluffs, as laid out and recorded, embraces a part of section 8, 9, 16, 17. It has a good steamboat landing, is improving considerably, and bids fair to make quite a business point.[92]

Rock Bluffs is estimated to have had about 5 houses at the time of survey. Probably, both Kanoshe and Rock Bluffs functioned primarily as market places for the farmers in their hinterlands. Farmhouses dotted the countryside around Rock Bluffs and there were a few in the vicinity of Kanoshe.[93] The settlers found large groves with good building timber on the Missouri bluffs, and a saw mill was being erected at a mill site about one-half mile from the mouth of Rock Creek.

In April, 1856, the surveyor described Ft. Calhoun in this manner, "The town of Ft. Calhoun situated in the northeast corner of the township on section 11 has a beautiful site and contains 8 houses and others are fast being built giving the appearance of rapid advancement."[94] Indeed, Ft. Calhoun did have several circumstances that favored its rapid advancement. Important advantages of this locality were the ample supply of timber and the good farming land that sustained 8 or 10 farmhouses in its hinterland.[95] These farmers became an important sector of its market. In this township, there was timber of construction quality that was milled at a steam saw mill erected here in 1856. Another major asset of this hamlet was the presence of a hotel, a 24 by 48 foot structure of hewn logs.[96] Ft. Calhoun was unique among hamlets because it was the only one with a hotel. Yet, since this hamlet was several miles from the Missouri River, its steamboat landing was rather

92 U.S.L.S., *op. cit.*, T11N, R14E, April 5-May 8, 1856.
93 *Ibid.*
94 U.S.L.S., *op. cit.*, T17N, R12E, March 26-April 14, 1856.
95 *Ibid.*
96 Andreas, *op. cit.*, p. 1471.

inconveniently located. Probably, this hotel was frequently used mainly by the traveling public that followed the wagon road between DeSoto and Florence. Another asset of this hamlet was its courthouse, which functioned as county seat of Washington County until 1858.[97]

In November, 1857, Central City was described in the following manner by the surveyor, "Section 34 has been selected as a townsite known as Central City. There are two good buildings, a store, and a dwelling, now erected on the townsite."[98] This hamlet that depended mainly on trade with the farmers of its hinterland had several major drawbacks to its location. The land around Central City was chiefly bottom. The same source indicated that in extremely high water the Missouri River overflows most of the land. Consequently, field cultivation was always a hazardous undertaking because crops were likely to be flooded. Moreover, this hamlet was located on the river bank, and consequently, it might be either flooded or eroded away.

The surveyor had little to say about Decatur during August, 1857, except this: "The town of Decatur has been laid out about one year, has an excellent steamboat landing, two stores, and 8 or 10 dwelling houses, but does not look thrifty".[99] There seems to have been two main reasons why Decatur did not look thrifty. First, like most hamlets, Decatur depended largely upon rural trade for its sustenance. However, the township waas not particularly suited for rural settlement because there was little timber and much of the land was broken and rated as second class for cultivation.[100] Secondly, the Omaha Indian Reservation bordered Decatur on the north. Not included within the public domain, this reservation was unavailable for pioneer settlement. Trade with these Indians was conducted mainly at the trading houses of Sarpy and Lambert instead of Decatur.

The German speaking hamlet of Frankfort was placed beside the Missouri River in the northwest corner of the study area only a few miles east of Niobrara. Frankfort was a farm-oriented community with 3 cabins in 1858.[101] It was surrounded by a small cluster of farmhouses

---

97 *Ibid.*
98 U.S.L.S., *op. cit.* T22N, R11E, November 22-25, 1857.
99 U.S.L.S., *op. cit.*, T24N, R10E, August 26, 1857.
100 *Ibid.*
101 U.S.L.S., *op. cit.*, T33N, R11E, March 19-27, 1856.

and a few fields. Beside it, another German settlement called Topeota had one townhouse. In the western Platte Valley, Grand Island, another German community was located near the western fringe of early settlement. These rural communities were the only settlements in eastern Nebraska that the surveyors mentioned specifically as being German. Their distinctiveness was maintained, at least for a short time, because they were cohesive groups on the western fringes of early settlement.

Elkhorn was settled by pioneers who were attracted to the site of a heavily traveled ferry crossing of the Elkhorn River. Here, many emigrants who were headed for the Platte Valley from Florence, Omaha City, or Bellevue, crossed this river. In 1856,"as yet but one house had been built," was the contemporary report.[102] Nevertheless, Elkhorn was situated in country where farmers were plowing and improving their claims. The bottomland of the Elkhorn River was subject to overflow, but the uplands provided excellent prairie grass and field sites.[103] Cottonwood was plentiful along the river banks, and the bluffs contained several small groves of oak, elm, and walnut.

Other than Indian villages and encampments, Buffalo was the only present or former settlement on the south side of the Platte River identified by the surveyors. It included only "one house in 1857, and it had no inhabitants.[104] From a site on the river bluffs about 250 feet above the bank, it commanded a panoramic view of 20 to 30 miles".[105] Scattered along the bluffs, a variety of trees included cedar, lynn, burr oak, walnut, hickory, and hackberry.

In late 1857, Buchanan, according to the surveyor, contained two houses, and it became the seat of Platte County.[106] It was place don the route of the Platte at the mouth of Shell Creek. This site enabled Buchanan to seize the opportunity for trade not only with the four neighboring farmsteads that lined the wagon road in the township, but also with the emigrants. Most emigrants who entered Nebraska joined the route of the Platte before reaching this hamlet. In order to capitalize

---

102 U.S.L.S., *op. cit.* T16N, R10E, May 14-June 2, 1856.
103 *Ibid.*
104 U.S.L.S., *op. cit.*, T17N, R7E, September 25-October 12, 1857.
105 *Ibid.*
106 U.S.L.S., *op. cit.* T17N, R4E, November 17-December 3, 1857.

more fully on the advantages of their site, the inhabitants of Buchanan proposed a toll bridge across Shell Creek.[107] Natural resources near Buchanan included fertile terrace soil and timber, particularly elm and cottonwood along the river channels.

Excluding the Platte Valley, the outlying territory, and hence the country west of the Missouri River Valley and its lower tributaries, was essentially devoid of nucleated settlement. South of the Platte River, two very small settlements were laid out less than 25 miles west of Nebraska City along the headward portion of the Little Nemaha River. The hamlet of Saltville included, according to the surveyor, "two buildings on the town site", but Syracuse had only "one dwelling in town",[108] and consequently can not be considered a hamlet.

Platted Townsites. Platted townsites, or paper towns that were entered on the surveyors' plats were laid out primarily as promotional ventures by speculators who hoped to profit from the sale of town lots. In some places, speculation on farm land and promotion of town property was very profitable. The following statement of August, 1856, indicates that greater gains were realized from townsite promotion than from speculation on rural land. "Land purchased at government prices in a short time commands from $10.00 to $50.00. Town property increases in still greater ratio. Everything is done on the cash principle."[109]

The places preferred for townsite promotion were those sites considered by speculators to be the most attractive for settlement. Promoters were lured especially to potential sites for river termini of railroads. Town promoters tried to anticipate where railroads would cross the Missouri River, and they predicted correctly that a railroad would follow the Platte Valley through Nebraska. They laid out some paper towns at ferry crossings of the Missouri and Platte rivers, and they placed others where rivers were forded on routes of migration. They placed other platted townsites in the suburbs of large towns and cities that were potential sites for residential or university centers. In some places, town promoters platted townsites among farmstead where rural trade was expected to generate town growth. Existing villages and hamlets along the Missouri River were too small to attract railroad

---

107 *The Nebraskian*, March 6, 1856.
108 U.S.L.S., *op. cit.* T8N, R10E, May 1-10, 1857.
109 *The Nebraskian*, August 13, 1856.

terminals. Consequently, paper towns could not attract them either. Furthermore, only a few river cities and towns wee fortunate enough to become important railroad termini.

Considering the small number of platted townsites which actually became towns, it may be concluded that most attempts at townsite promotion were unsuccessful. For example, the surveyors recorded 18 paper towns, four of which have survived to the present: Otoe, Palmyra, West Point, and Blue Springs (Appendix B). Consequently, there has been approximately an 80 per cent decline in the numbers of these paper towns since the time of original land survey.[110]

Interpretation of the Distribution of Nucleated Settlements

Among their records in the field notes and on the plats, the surveyors often neglected to tell whether or not river towns were served by ferries and steamboat landings. In fact, at 16 Missouri River towns that they described, the surveyors did not record either ferries or steamboats; nor did they mention their absence. In some instances, entries from contemporary newspapers provided this kind of information. Nevertheless, the surveyors did record twelve steamboat landings. Furthermore, there were both ferries and steamboat landings at eight river towns. These towns included Dakota City, DeSoto, Omaha City, Kearney City, Nebraska City, Brownville, Cuming, and St. Deroin. Also, Nebraska City was linked directly by wagon road with Bennett's Ferry, a crossing south of Nebraska City that did not have a steamboat landing. Niobrara, St. Calhoun, Decatur, and Rock Bluff were said to have had steamboat landings; the surveyors did not record ferries near them. Figure 4 shows the location of steamboat landings and ferries recorded by the surveyors.

Although townsite promoters were attracted often to ferry sites, ferry crossings were relatively subordinate factors in bringing about the

---

110 Those paper towns from the survey that have vanished include: LaPlatte, Mount Vernon, St. Stephens, Papillion, Mt. Pleasant, Vernona, Farmington, Pacific City, Chester, Clagtona, Austin, Franklin, Emerson, and Nenagh.

growth of river settlements. The following paper townsites were located at ferry crossings of the Missouri River: LaPlatte, St. Stephens, Lewis, Bennetts, and Lobsingers. Furthermore, there was not any settlement where the Hawke and Dillon ferry crossed the Missouri River. The surveyors recorded 19 ferries. The zone of dense ferry crossings (11 ferries) extended from DeSoto to Brownville. Here, wagon roads led from the ferries directly to the cities and large towns. Ferries were spaced somewhat less densely (6 ferries) from Brownville to the extreme southeast corner of Nebraska, and here, they crossed where there were no towns. In fact, one third of the Missouri ferries crossed at some distance from river towns. Ferries were not particularly significant to the growth of river towns, unless they happened to serve river towns with heavily used steamboat landings. By themselves, ferries did not impose the necessity for special bulk-breaking or changes in carriers.

Along the south Missouri River, compact settlements were placed on rolling upland sites that were not far from where the channel impinged against the Nebraska bluffs. On the other hand, along the northern Missouri Valley, most river towns were located on well drained terraces at the edge of the channel, although some were located on flood plains that were subject to overflow or washout. With channel-side sites, these compact settlements had the advantage of proximity to their steamboat landings. A few river towns of the northern Missouri Valley had terrace sites that were more distant from the channel. Ponca was two miles away. Takama was five miles away. DeSoto was one fourth of a mile from the channel, and Ft. Calhoun was a mile and a half away. Although somewhat distant from the river, these river towns had access by wagon roads to their steamboat landings.

Having 50 to 200 houses, cities and large towns occupied a zone between Florence and Nebraska City that straddled the mouth of the Platte River. Specializing in emigrant outfitting, these Missouri River settlements served as intervening places for trade and manufacture along direct routes of migration between the Missouri Valley and Fort Kearney. Including about three fifths of the agglomerated houses that were tallied from the survey and estimated from the 1860 census, the size of these large settlements was related to their importance as commercial cross-route sites where ferries and steamboat landings coincided. Here, the settlers outfitted the emigrants and developed economies that depended upon imported merchandise, largely from St. Louis.[111] The paramount reason for the flourishing growth of cities and large towns was their function as outfitting centers.

The early growth of cities and large towns evolved from the early establishment of several features, including overwintering quarters for the Mormons, fur trading posts, county courthouses, the Territorial capital, freight line headquarters, and warehouses for outfitting emigrants. Florence, formerly called Winter Quarters, began as an overwintering place for the Mormons, and later it became an outfitting center for them.[112] Bellevue grew at the site of the post of the old North West Fur Company. Furthermore, it was promoted by acquisition of the Cass County courthouse.[113] Omaha City flourished after it was selected as the Territorial capital. Its selection was encouraged by business interests in Council Bluffs, Iowa, because they knew that both cities would benefit if Omaha City became the headquarters of the Pacific Telegraph Company and the Union Pacific Railroad Company.[114] Nebraska City was promoted by prominent business men, and special advantages were gained for it by residents who were influential in the Territorial legislature.[115] Generally, cities and large towns offered provisions for the emigrants, and they provided many services that included the bulk-breaking of steamboat freight, the warehousing of supplies, the outfitting of wagon trains, and the repair and manufacture of equipment. Moreover, Omaha City and Nebraska City gained a share of their sustenance from the headquarters of freight lines to Denver and elsewhere to the West.[116] Furthermore, cities and large towns lured many newcomers to settle by offering them job opportunities and personal conveniences.[117]

From Iowa, many routes of migration entered the Missouri Valley and crossed the river at more than 15 ferries. Upon entering Territorial Nebraska, routes of migration converged into cities and large towns, from which most overland routes led toward Fort Kearney; but one led

---

111 Graebner, *op. cit.*, pp. 213-214.
112 *The Nebraskian*, July 23, 1856.
113 *Bellevue Gazette*, October 1, 1857.
114 *The Huntsman's Echo*, July 26, 1860.
115 *Nebraska News*, December 19, 1857.
116 Andreas, A. T., *op. cit.*, p. 1203.
117 *Nebraska Advertiser*, August 23, 1856.

to Marysville, Kansas (Figure 4). At the time of original land survey, Omaha City and Nebraska City were the cities (of 100 to 200 houses) from which wagon roads led directly to Fort Kearney. Large towns (of 50 to 99 houses) were located also to direct routes to Fort Kearney. Here, for example, Florence, Bellevue, and Plattsmouth served as outfitting centers (Figure 6). Before railroads reached the Missouri River, emigrants who crossed into Nebraska on ferries located north of Florence or south of Nebraska City often followed wagon roads that converged into the urbanized zone between Florence and Nebraska City before heading to Fort Kearney. For example, a wagon road led from Brownville to Nebraska City before it continued to Fort Kearney. Also from Dakota, emigrants traveled to Florence or Omaha City before heading westward. The convenience of this reach of the Missouri Valley for emigrants who outfitted and debarked directly toward Fort Kearney accounts probably for the growth of cities and large towns there.

Outside the zone where direct debarkation to Fort Kearney took place, citations from newspapers and reports of the surveyors revealed that emigrant outfitting supported only two small towns (of 25 to 49 houses) along the Missouri Valley. Outside this zone, only Dakota[118] and Brownville[119] included sufficient industry and enough commercial diversity to indicate that they were minor places for the outfitting of emigrants. Here, commercial establishments included banks, grocery stores, drug stores, general stores, dry goods stores, and warehouses from which imported goods were distributed. Mechanics' shops that served the emigrants included harness shops, blacksmith shops and wagon makers' shops. Furthermore, both small towns were served by heavily traveled ferries that crossed the Missouri River.

Along the Platte Valley, the minor refitting of emigrants who had been outfitted previously was carried on at two villages (of 10 to 24 houses) that held general stores, and trade with the emigrants helped support another general store at Fort Kearney (Figure 6). At the villages of Fremont and Columbus, some emigrants refitted themselves with equipment that was overlooked in the Missouri Valley, and others took on provisions that were in short supply. Finally, on the west edge of Fort Kearney Military Reservation, emigrants found at a general store their

---

118 *Dakota City Herald*, November 26, 1859.
119 *Nebraska Advertiser*, June 7, 1856.

last stop for provisions along the central route of migration through the Platte Valley.[120] Emigrants who traveled through the Platte Valley provided only enough trade to support villages because fewer settlers and fewer provisions were needed to refit the emigrants than to outfit them.[121]

Within the Missouri Valley, a considerable share of the trade at most villages and small towns came from travelers who stayed at hotels (Figure 6). Except for Brownville other small towns and villages were located north of the zone of direct embarkation to Fort Kearney, probably because of the few emigrants who traveled westward from this stretch of river. Within the northern Missouri Valley, the arrangement of small river settlements favored the accommodation of travelers along the Nebraska side of the Missouri Valley. These travelers were boarded and lodged at hotels that were often called "houses". A brief description of such a house follows:

> The Bates House was a hotel for boarders and the traveling public. The prices of board and other fares have been reduced. Nowhere can the traveler get so much for his money. Fluids at the bar are of good quality. His table is well supplied and the hotel is clean.[122]

Although most villages and small towns had one hotel, some included two hotels, and others had none. For example, the village of Ponca welcomed travelers at the Barrett's House and the Ponca House.[123] On the other hand, the village of Harney and the small towns of Logan and St. Johns did not have hotels. Although lacking hotels, these three urban settlements were situated in the vicinity of Dakota, where travelers were housed at the Bates House and the Chihuahua House.[124] With the exception of Dakota and Brownville, villages and small towns along the Missouri Valley had infrequent dealings with emigrants. They did not function as outfitting centers because they

---

120 U.S.L.S., *op. cit.*, T8N, R15W, August 25, 1859.
121 *The Nebraskian*, March 5, 1856.
122 *Dakota City Herald*, August 13, 1859.
123 *Dakota City Herald*, January 7, 1860.
124 *Dakota City Herald*, November 26, 1859.

lacked the necessary banks, the necessary warehouses, and a sufficient variety of commercial establishments. Furthermore, many of them were so far from the channel that they had neither steamboat landings nor ferry crossings on the Missouri River. Ferries did not cross this river west of Dakota, and there was no regular ferry service at urban settlements between Dakota and Cuming.[125]

Although most villages were laid out along routes that were frequented by emigrants and local travelers, it can be presumed that hamlets (with 2 to 10 houses) were sustained primarily by local trade with rural settlers of their hinterlands. Of the eleven hamlets, more than half were placed along the Missouri Valley where steamboat landings provided four hamlets, St. Deroin, Rock Bluffs, Ft. Calhoun, and Decatur, with access to goods from St. Louis, Missouri (Figure 4). It may be presumed that the general stores at these hamlets were stocked with imported provisions that were sold to the rural settlers. From the country-side, the settlers sent to the hamlets grain for their grist mills and timber for their saw mills. Among these hamlets of the Missouri Valley were Nemaha, Kenoshe, Rock Bluffs, St. Deroin, Decatur, and Frankfort. Finally, Archer, Salem, and Falls City traded with the farmers of the Muddy and Big Nemaha valleys where they were located. A few hamlets gained a substantial share of their trade from travelers. Inasmuch as Ft. Calhoun was placed a few miles from the river, its steamboat landing was inconvenient. Yet, Ft. Calhoun had a hotel. Presumably, this hotel received a share of its trade from river travelers who stayed there.[126] At the ferry crossing of the Elkhorn River, Elkhorn gained much of its income from the travelers who frequented the McNeal House and the Pike's Peak House[127] (Figure 6).

Along the Union Pacific Railroad, the fate of urban settlements was determined when the railroad company decided upon its route through the Platte Valley. The original site of Fremont was located close to a large timbered island in the Platte River; and the site of Columbus was chosen at the ferry crossing of the Loup Fork River. Fremont and Columbus still exist because the railroad joined them. However, Buchanan, and Fontenelle vanished because they were bypassed. When

---

125 *The Nebraskian*, August 20, 1856.
126 *The Nebraskian*, July 23, 1856.
127 *Huntsman's Echo*, September 6, 1860.

the Union Pacific Railroad caused cities and large towns to lose their roles as outfitting centers for emigrants, Platte settlements attempted to acquire new roles as trade centers for the agricultural population of their hinterlands, and they started to increase the export of agricultural commodities to the East.

Regardless of the changing technology in transportation that resulted in the ebb and flow of commerce from one place to another, the judicial and administrative functions of county seats provided the thread of continuity that permitted these settlements to endure. Nucleated settlements that acquired county seats during the period of original survey evidenced a greater degree of permanence than those urban settlements that were without them. Twelve of the 16 compact settlements that were county seats at the time of survey exist today.[128] All cities and all large towns that became county seats have endured. Fontenelle was the only one of the four small towns with a county seat that disappeared. Similarly, only one of the three villages that were county seats vanished. This was St. James. Moreover, only two of the five hamlets that were county seats disappeared. They were Archer and Buchanan. On the other hand, only five of the twenty-three compact settlements that did not become county seats before the land survey have persisted. None of the large towns or small towns that lacked county seats during the period of survey exist today. Logan, Omadi, St. Johns, Florence, Kearney City, and South Nebraska City have either disappeared or have been incorporated into other agglomerated settlements. Only two of the five villages that were not mentioned in the survey or newspapers as being county seats at the time of survey, remain today. Columbus and Fremont exist; DeSoto, Harney, and Cuming have vanished. Finally, of the 12 hamlets that lacked county courthouses, only three exist now. Those that have persisted are Nemaha, Decatur, and Palmyra. Whereas, 75 per cent of nucleated settlements that held county seats at the time of survey remain today, only 22 per cent of the urban settlements that were not county seats still exist.

Before the panic of 1857, the quickest way for pioneers to acquire wealth was to gain the unearned increments that were created by the spiraling prices of urban real estate. Although a settler could pre-empt

---

128 Omaha City, Nebraska City, Bellevue, Plattsmouth, Tekama, Brownville, Dakota City, Ponca, Niobrara, Salem, Falls City, and Ft. Calhoun.

only a single 160 acre unit of land in the country, he could purchase several urban lots and retain them for the purpose of speculation on their future worth. As stated earlier, generally, the price of town property inflated at a much faster rate than the price of land in the country.[129] The sharp increase in the price of city lots led to very brisk speculation. With the establishment of an emigrant line from the East to Marysville, Kansas, via Nebraska City, the price of city lots advanced 50 per cent.[130] In the business district of Omaha City, the prices of lots were $1,000 to $2,000, and during 1856, the prices of lots increased 50 per cent above those of the previous year.[131] Land speculation was an activity in which hundreds of settlers took part at urban settlements and platted townsites. Pioneers purchased lots, made improvements, and sold them at a profit in towns of eastern Nebraska. Furthermore, the sale of urban property was a source of livelihood for many lot agents, lawyers, and surveyors.[132] Often, townsites were platted as a means of speculation at potential railroad termini along the Missouri River. In fact, there were more speculative paper towns than actual urban settlements at the time of original land survey. The governor's message of December 19, 1857, described the effects of the panic of 1857, attributing it to extravagant speculation and unsound banking practices:

> To the country at large, the past year has been truly eventful. A disastrous monetary revulsion, delayed for a time by western gold discoveries, had befallen us at last-prostrating credit-destroying confidence-ruining individual and associated capitalists-disclosing monstrous frauds and bringing distress, penury, and beggery. It is estimated that about two thirds of the currency of the country is debt. The cause has been the private speculation and the excesses of an insecure banking system.[133]

After the panic of 1857, the speculation bubble was broken, and the interest in speculation on town lots and on platted townsites declined.[134]

---

129 *The Nebraskian*, August 13, 1856.
130 *Nebraska Advertiser*, August 16, 1856.
131 *Ibid.*
132 *Ibid.*
133 *Nebraska News*, December 19, 1857.
134 Andreas, A. T., *op. cit.*, p. 692.

The urban settlements were built rapidly during the early years of the Territorial period, and consequently construction became a major industry for the pioneers. From the start, pioneers at nucleated settlements engaged in primary manufacturing. Timber, rather than minerals, was utilized for the construction of most houses and other buildings. Steam saw mills were among the earliest features. Commonly, cities and large towns had 2 or 3 steam saw mills, and some settlements received lumber from portable saw mills that were located in nearby groves of timber. Some hamlets and most villages had saw mills (Figure 3).[135] Furthermore, some large urban settlements imported machines for manufacturing shingles. In addition to processing local hardwoods, many urban settlements supplemented local deficiencies with pine lumber that was imported by steamboat.[136] For example, at Brownville in 1856, the local supply of lumber could not keep up with the rate of house construction.[137] Although lumber was the mainstay, bricks and limestone blocks were used for the construction of wells and some buildings. At Omaha City and Nebraska City, brick kilns wee supplied with clay from local pits. Quarried from valley outcroppings, limestone was used for the construction of a few large buildings.[138] The Omaha Mission building was built of limestone blocks. Lime kilns were common features at large settlements. An important product, quick lime was the major ingredient of plaster. As ingredients for concrete, sand and gravel were extracted from borrow pits, like the one a mile south of Nebraska City. The construction industry employed many mechanics and general laborers. These mechanics included sawyers, painters, plasterers, bricklayers, carpenters, and stone cutters. Because laborers and mechanics of all kinds were in short supply, many settlers were obliged to build their own homes. At Brownville, for example, the houses were reported to have given the appearance of hasty construction.[139]

135 Survey records show that about one-third of the hamlets and about two-thirds of the villages had saw mills.
136 *Bellevue Gazette*, October 23, 1856.
137 *Ibid*.
138 *Ibid*.
139 *Nebraska Advertiser*, June 21, 1856.

CHAPTER V

DISPERSED SETTLEMENT

First, this chapter describes various types of dispersed dwellings and agricultural features that the surveyors identified within the rural landscape. Then, it presents the distribution of farmsteads, fields, and other agricultural features that were recorded. Following this, patterns of extractive features such as saw mills, limestone quarries, lime kilns, coal mines, and salt vats are presented. Next, samples of farmhouse patterns are described from plats believed to be representative of the overall pattern of settlement. Finally, as revealed by the original land survey, dispersed settlement is interpreted.

Dispersed dwellings portrayed the overall pattern of settlement in Nebraska Territory because they were the most widespread features of settlement. The surveyors used eleven different terms to describe different kinds of dispersed dwellings (Table 6). Forty per cent of them were described as houses, and 23 per cent were recorded as cabins. There were six ranches, and two dwellings were called shanties.

The total of 464 dispersed dwellings, including 380 that were tallied from the survey and 84 houses that were estimated from surveyors' terms to have been observed by surveyors, were considerably fewer than the number of houses that are believed to have been present in the area of study. As stated previously, surveyors could not see all farmhouses that were located in section interiors from lines of the survey. Furthermore, it is important to recognize limitations that the brief duration of survey imposed upon the nature of the survey records.

TABLE 6

REGIONAL TABULATION OF DISPERSED SETTLEMENT

Features[1]	Eastern Nebraska Territory	South Missouri Valley	North Missouri Valley	East Platte Valley	West Platte Valley	Outlying Territory
House	153	85	13	22	32	1
Log House	42	35	0	7	0	0
Log Cabin	7	6	0	0	0	1
Cabin	32	17	9	5	0	1
Shanty	2	2	0	0	0	0
Stone House	1	1	0	0	0	0
Ranch	6	1	0	0	4	1
Settler	149	76	6	39	2	26
Stage Station	4	0	0	0	2	2
Trading Post	7	0	2	0	2	3
Post Office	4	1	0	0	3	0
Total	407	224	30	73	45	35

In each township, surveyors observed only those features of settlement that were visible to them during the short interval required for completion of survey, usually about one week. Rarely did surveyors see a complete pioneer landscape because pioneering was an on-going process, and surveyors observed usually the initial phase of this process. For example, compare the landscape along the wagon road northwest of Logan in March 10-13, 1858, when the surveyor recorded it, with two years later, in 1860, when a newspaper reporter described it. In 1858, there was no mention of any rural settlers northwest of Logan,

1   This tabulation of dispersed features included 380 dwelling houses of different types as well as stage stations, trading posts, and post offices. It excludes those estimates of dispersed dwellings for occupied townships where surveyors omitted exact counts.

although timber was shown on the plat there. The only settlers that surveyors recorded in this area were in Logan. All that the surveyor said was: "The original site of the town of Logan is in the northwest corner of the township in section 6 [T28N, R9E]. It contains 30 houses and is immediately on the bank of the Missouri River." However, in 1860, the rural landscape to the northwest of Logan was portrayed in this thumb nail sketch:

> Northwesterly for one mile [from Logan] we were in the Logan Timber. Here, a saw mill was puffing and blowing while men navigated logs into it and lumber out of it. Then, we went nearly west as curves of the road would permit. On either side were snug houses on every half mile of ground, up and down the bottom as far as the eye could reach. Standing in the rear, or off to one side of nearly all, were stacks of hay and grain; and each house had its crib of corn handy in which bushels could be counted by the hundred.[2]

This comparison illustrates the rapidity of land transformation along the Missouri Valley during the Territorial period from essentially natural conditions to a landscape of pioneering.

In their records, surveyors identified 50 log dwellings, which were located mostly in the southeast corner of the study area (Figure 9). Here, log dwellings were distributed in linear patterns along the Muddy Creek and the Big Nemaha River. Elsewhere along the Missouri Valley, they were included among farmhouses around Omaha City, Nebraska City, St. Deroin, Niobrara, and Frankfort. Some log dwellings were located along the route of the Platte near Elkhorn and Buchanan. Furthermore, two log cabins were placed along Beaver Creek, and one was recorded in the Elkhorn Valley. Generally, log cabins were built in rural areas, far from the nearest saw mills. Except at Omaha City, Nebraska City, and Salem, log cabins were not identified in the hinterlands of towns that had saw mills.

Although mostly farmers, a few dispersed dwellers were engaged in other occupations. Besides farmhouses, there were seven trading posts. They were located chiefly near Indian reservations like the Omaha,

---

2   *Dakota City Herald*, January 7, 1860.

the Otoe, and the Missouri. Furthermore, four stage stations were spaced at wide intervals along wagon roads through the western part of the Platte Valley and along cutoff routes south of the Platte Valley. Generally occurring at compact settlements, three post offices served rural population in the east Platte Valley, and one served a rural area in the south Missouri Valley.

Erected during 1867, this log cabin was removed from a pioneer claim in southeastern Nebraska to the Homestead National Monument near Beatrice.

Kinds of Agricultural Features

In eastern Nebraska, features that were associated with agriculture included: fields, wells, stables, fences, gardens, corn cribs, hay stacks, smoke houses, and several types of cabins and houses. Three stables were recorded at ranches in the eastern part of the Platte Valley,[3] and two barns were noted at farms within the south Missouri Valley.[4] Surveyors recorded only one smokehouse, although they were probably more common. It was built on a farmstead in the south Missouri Valley.[5] Two years after the date of survey, a newspaper reporter observed many corn cribs and haystacks along the wagon road northwest of Logan.[6] Two wells were noted in the west Platte Valley, and a windmill was recorded that probably had another well associated with it.[7] These wells were hand dug on the bottomland of the Platte River where water could be reached at depths of only 10 to 15 feet.

The fences that were recorded on the township plats usually enclosed crops of corn, as shown on the plats, and consequently, their purpose was apparently to fence out livestock that grazed the common prairie. However, most fields that the surveyors recorded were unfenced or records of fencing were omitted. Only 49 fields that have been tallied were fenced, representing only one tenth of the total number of fields shown on township plats. Certainly, many fences went unobserved by surveyors, particularly those surrounding fields that were located within section interiors. Probably, most fences were built of rails or poles, although fencing materials were rarely specified by surveyors. About three fourths of the 49 fences within eastern Nebraska Territory were located in the south Missouri Valley. Here six sod fences were constructed also.[8] Another sod fence was recorded by surveyors from the Platte Valley.

In the process of rural settlement, the sequence of construction for some features on claims undoubtedly varied, and the periods of development for many features probably overlapped. Nor were all features of pioneer farms necessarily present on any particular claim. For example, only about 10 per cent of pioneer claims had fields that were fenced at the time of survey. Furthermore, many claims in the vicinity

3   Stables were located in T14N, R5W; T11N, R9W; and T15N, R3W.
4   Barns were observed in T15N, R13E; and T11N, R14E.
5   The smokehouse was located in T12N, R14E.
6   *Dakota City Herald*, January 7, 1860.
7   Wells were located in T11N, R9W; T10N, R11W; Windmill in T10N, R10W.
8   Sod fences: T17N, R7E; T17N, R8E; T10N, R13E; T11N, R13E; T15N, R13E; and T14N, R14E.

of cities and large towns along the Missouri River were reported not to have had farmhouses on them. However, in most cases, the sequence of rural settlement appears to have been as follows: claim, house-building, sod-breaking, fencing, and corn-planting. Evidence for this sequence of development has been derived from associations of features as recorded by surveyors, and from the following entry in a Territorial newspaper.

> *Prairie Breaking.* Everyone who has a claim is getting from ten to one hundred acres done, the most of which is planted to corn. The crop will pay for breaking and land besides in one season.[9]

This statement indicates that claims were established first, followed by breaking of prairie and then planting of corn. Of course, this sequence of rural settlement does not include house-building or fencing. An alternative to building a farm house at the onset seems to have been presumably temporary residence in a town.

If newcomers who intended to settle in eastern Nebraska did not settle immediately at compact settlements, their first undertaking was to locate claims of 160 acres and to record them at the local Land Office. Then, in order to pre-empt and hold claims, usually, pioneer farmers built farmhouses on them. Having built their homes, they improved their claims by breaking sod, commonly about 10 to 20 acres. It was necessary for pioneers to plant corn within a fairly short interval of time. Fence building could either precede or follow soon after planting of corn. Apparently, fences were built primarily to protect growing crops from livestock damage. Many fields of corn along wagon roads in the hinterlands of Missouri River cities and large towns were not accompanied by farmhouses. Possibly, such fields belonged to part-time farmers who lived in river towns while farming their crops on claims along wagon roads that led to town; or they belonged to farmers who resided temporarily in town. This practice permitted a delay in construction of farmhouses. From this observation, it is inferred that farmhouses were built last in the sequence of settlement on these claims. Here, the most likely sequence of development was: claim, breaking, fencing, or corn planting and then fencing, and farmhouse building.

---

9   *The Nebraskian,* May 21, 1856.

Of course, in this sequence, fencing of early pioneer fields was omitted commonly, as was the construction of farmhouses. As stated previously, only about 10 per cent of the fields recorded by surveyors were shown as fenced or enclosed, or so described. The kind of fencing was not characterized, generally, except for a few sod fences.

Distribution of Dispersed Settlement

Based mainly upon survey records, only about 30 per cent of early settlement in eastern Nebraska was dispersed. However, according to assumptions already made, the number of dispersed dwellings recorded by surveyors was under-represented by about 37 per cent. Increasing by 37 per cent the 464 houses that were recorded in the survey and estimated for plats not having exact house counts provides a total estimate of about 636 dispersed dwellings. As a result, the estimated proportion of dispersed dwellings in the total population of houses is about 40 per cent. Of the 464 dispersed dwellings derived from field notes and plats, 252 dwellings, or more than 50 per cent, were located in the south Missouri Valley (Table 7). Here, either they formed linear patterns along tributaries of the Missouri Valley, or they formed clusters in the vicinity of compact settlements (Figure 6). Five to ten farmhouses were clustered near most compact settlements, but the size of each cluster did not correspond with its associated settlement. For example, clusters of the same size were grouped near hamlets like Archer, Nemaha, Salem, and St. Deroin as well as near cities and large towns like Omaha City, Nebraska City, Bellevue, and Plattsmouth. Farmhouses that formed linear patterns were distributed along the middle and lower reaches of the following valleys: Papillion, Weeping Water, Little Nemaha, Muddy, and Big Nemaha. A linear pattern of four farmhouses occurred along the middle reach of the Little Papillion Creek. Another 11 farmhouses paralleled Weeping Water Valley for a distance of eight miles from Nebraska City. Northwest of Nemaha, 15 farmhouses stretched out for the same number of miles along the Little Nemaha Valley. Along the valley of Muddy Creek, 11 farmhouses extended northwest of Archer. Northwest of Salem, 18 farmhouses occurred for 20 miles along the Long Branch of the Big Nemaha River. Finally, 10 farmhouses were placed east of Salem along the Big

Nemaha. The only dispersed dwelling other than farmhouses in this subregion was the Three Groves Post Office located about 10 miles west of Kanoshe.

TABLE 7

REGIONAL MEASURES OF DISPERSED SETTLEMENT

Areas of Settlement	Total Dwellings[10]	Per cent of Dispersed Dwellings[11]	Per cent Rural[12]	Dispersed Density Per Settled Township[13]
South Missouri	252	55	25	5
North Missouri	40	9	13	2
East Platte	76	16	50	4
West Platte	57	12	100	4
Outlying Territory	39	8	93	2
Eastern Nebraska	464	100	30	4

In the northern Missouri Valley, the approximately 40 dispersed dwellings represented only about 9 per cent of those recorded by surveyors in eastern Nebraska (Table 7). Farmhouses were clustered around a few hamlets, but they were absent from hinterlands of most villages and small towns. Farmhouses were not laid out in linear patterns, except four along the Niobrara River, and four others along the Missouri River east of Tekama. In the north Missouri Valley, Niobrara

10 Includes the 380 dispersed dwellings tallied from the survey records and 84 houses estimated by numerical translation of descriptive terms from the original field notes.
11 The proportion of all dispersed dwellings within eastern Nebraska that are computed for each area of settlement.
12 The ratio of the number of dispersed dwellings within each area of settlement to total number of dwellings there.
13 Equals the number of dispersed dwellings within each area of settlement divided by the number of townships that were settled there.

with six farmhouses, Frankfort with nine farmhouses, and Decatur with two farmhouses, were the only settlements having small clusters of farmhouses in their hinterlands. Near the Omaha Reservation and Decatur, two trading posts were included among this small cluster of dispersed dwellings.

The east Platte Valley had 76 farmhouses that represented about 15 per cent of dispersed settlement recorded in eastern Nebraska. These farmhouses were dispersed mainly in a linear pattern along the military wagon road on the left back of the Platte River between Columbus and Fremont. Here, each settled township had on the average about four dispersed dwellings. Besides this primary pattern, there were two secondary linear patterns in the east Platte Valley. One string of farmhouses was placed along Maple Creek due west of Fontenelle, and the other secondary linear pattern paralleled Shell Creek along a road that linked with Columbus, a few miles to the south. Elsewhere in this subregion, there were a few farmhouses along the Elkhorn Valley near the ferry crossing and a few along the Loup River east of the Pawnee Reservation.

In the west Platte Valley, 57 dwellings represented about 12 per cent of dispersed settlement that surveyors recorded in eastern Nebraska. Primarily, this dispersed settlement formed a linear pattern along the wagon road beside the left bank of the Platte River (Figure 6). Although these dwellings were mostly farmhouses, there were among them two ranches, a stage station, a store, and two post offices. Furthermore, a railroad depot was located on the Union Pacific Railroad. This railroad had been built along the wagon road a short time before the survey. The wagon road that followed the right bank of the Platte River in this western subregion had only a few dispersed dwellings. Here, settlement included three farmhouses, a ranch, a stage station, and a store at the west edge of the Fort Kearney Military Reservation.

The outlying territory had 39 dispersed dwellings that represented only about 8 per cent of those recorded by surveyors. The majority were farmhouses located in a few small clusters (Figure 6). Two clusters were located in the Salt Creek Valley; one about 12 miles northeast of the site of Lincoln and the other about 12 miles to the southeast of this townsite. Another small cluster of farmhouses was placed along Indian Creek, a tributary of the Big Blue River. North of the Platte Valley, a "large settlement" of undefined character was located in the middle reach of the Elkhorn Valley, and two small clusters of farmhouses were grouped along river valleys: one in Logan Valley and another in Aowa Valley. Elsewhere, a few stage stations were widely spaced along the cutoff routes to the Fort Kearney Military Reservation. Along the cutoff route that paralleled Beaver Creek, there were a stage station and a log cabin. And, along the cutoff route from Kansas that paralleled the Little Blue River, there were two trading posts, one of which was near the Otoe and Missouri Reservation. Also along this route, there was an express station and the "Liberty Farm," possibly the residence of a flag-waving American or a shelter for freedom seeking slaves.

Distribution of Fields

Surveyors employed several terms to describe the cultivated land of pioneers. These terms included fields, breakings, improvement, plowed fields, and compound names for fields that included the specific crop. Of the 410 early fields about one half were recorded as fields, about 21 per cent were described as corn fields, about 19 per cent were reported as plowed fields, and about 7 per cent were noted as breakings. The use of the term "improvement" by surveyors was confined mainly to the west Platte Valley. Plowed fields were noted in all regions where land was cultivated. Generally, some cultivated land was identified as "fields". Corn fields were recorded largely within the south Missouri Valley and the Platte Valley. Besides corn fields, surveyors observed fields of wheat, potatoes, and buckwheat. A few fields of wheat were recorded in the south Missouri and east Platte valleys. A potato field was described in the south Missouri Valley, and finally, a buckwheat field was noted in the east Platte Valley.[14]

As stated earlier, pioneer fields were greatly underrepresented in section interiors by original land surveyors throughout most of the pattern of early fields (Figure 8). In eastern Nebraska, surveyors recorded 410 fields that included a total of about 2510 acres, a figure equivalent to almost nine sections of land. On the average, these fields held about six acres of cultivated land. However, they varied considerably

14 A potato field was located in T15N, R12E, and a buckwheat field was recorded in T17N, R1E.

in size. They ranged in size from small plots of one or two acres to a few "improvements" of 200 to 300 acres. The overall distribution of fields included two important acres: the Missouri Valley from Florence southward and, secondly, the Platte Valley along the wagon road between Fremont and the Grant Island Post Office (Figure 10).

In its southern half, the Missouri Valley had 263 fields, as reported by surveyors, that represented about two thirds of the fields in eastern Nebraska (Table 8). They were small, averaging about seven acres. The majority of fields were concentrated near large compact settlements in the zone of emigrant outfitting that extended between Florence and Nebraska City. A minority of them were cultivated along terraces of the Big Nemaha River and of the Muddy Creek. Fields of the south Missouri Valley were relatively small because most were located on sloping uplands where cultivation was more difficult for pioneers than on level land. By comparison, fields of the Platte Valley that were cultivated on nearly level benchland averaged about 30 acres in size. On uplands between Florence and Nebraska City, some fields accompanied farmhouses, but others were isolated along wagon roads in the hinterlands of these compact settlements. For example, one half of the fields were isolated from farmhouses in the hinterlands of Florence, Bellevue, Omaha City, and Plattsmouth. Also, fields in the vicinity of Kanoshe, Rock Bluffs, and Nebraska City were isolated along wagon roads there. In the south Missouri Valley, there were 44 more fields than farmhouses. Most of the isolated fields were located within ten miles or less from their nearest compact settlement. Perhaps, these 44 fields that were isolated along wagon roads were tilled by part-time farmers in the hinterland of river towns where they resided, or farmers may have started farming from town before building houses on their farms. In either case, the number of pioneers who engaged directly in early agriculture from Florence southward along the Missouri Valley was probably greater than the number of farmhouses indicated.

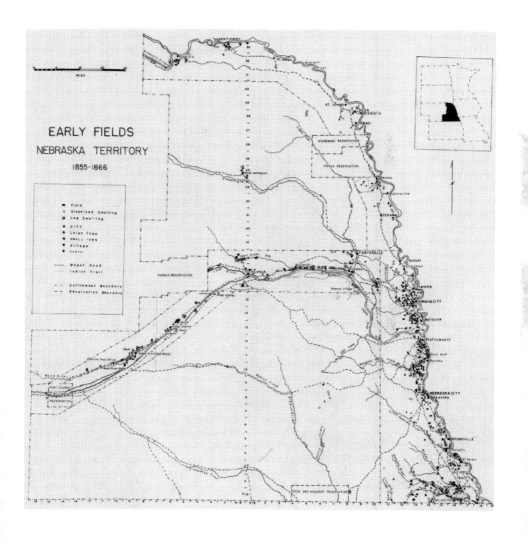

EARLY FIELDS
NEBRASKA TERRITORY
1855-1866

45

TABLE 8

REGIONAL MEASURES OF FIELDS

Areas of Settlement	Total Fields	Per cent of Total Fields[15]	Total Acreage	Per cent of Total Acreage[16]	Average Field Size (in acres)
South Missouri	263	66	2510	43	9
North Missouri	33	8	460	8	14
East Platte	61	15	1490	25	25
West Platte	41	9	1250	22	33
Outlying Territory	12	2	100	2	15
Eastern Nebraska	410	100	5810	100	14

In the north Missouri Valley, the 33 early fields represented only about eight per cent of those recorded in the area of study. In this subregion, the small percentage of fields was exceeded considerably by the proportion of farmhouses, about 20 per cent (Tables 7, 8). Perhaps, in this somewhat hilly terrain, surveyors may have missed more fields than houses. Here, as probably in many other localities, the settlement process was still under way. For example it was reported that settlers in three townships had made little improvement as yet except for building cabins.[17] On the other hand, the excess of farmhouses over fields may be related to the fact that, here, settlers were less involved with supply of emigrants and their livestock than were pioneers who lived in the zone between Nebraska City and Florence. Arranged in five clusters, about one half of the fields were isolated from farmhouses. Such was the case in the hinterlands of St. James, St. Johns, Omadi, Decatur, and Tekama. At these small compact settlements, part-time or town-based farmers

15 Percent of total fields means the proportion of all fields within eastern Nebraska computed for each area of settlement.
16 Per cent of total acreage means the proportion of all field acreage within eastern Nebraska computed for each area of settlement.
17 U.S.L.S., *op. cit.*, T33N, R2W, September 4-8, 1858.

commuted along wagon roads to isolated fields that they tilled. Most fields were located on terraces of the north Missouri Valley, a location that favored a larger size, about 15 acres, compared with smaller fields on uplands of the southern Missouri Valley.

In the east Platte Valley, as recorded by the surveyors, the 61 fields comprised about 15 per cent of those in eastern Nebraska. They were relatively large fields, averaging about 25 acres in size (Table 8). On terrace sites here as elsewhere, flatness of land facilitated cultivation of larger fields. In addition to the linear pattern of fields along the military wagon road, there were small clusters of five or six fields near Columbus and Fremont. Also, short strings of fields occurred along the following valleys north of the Platte: Shell Creek, Rawhide Creek, and Maple Creek. Most fields, although by no means all, were adjacent to their associated farmhouses.

In the west Platte Valley, the 41 fields, as reported by surveyors, included about 9 per cent of those in eastern Nebraska. Most fields were distributed along the military wagon road in two clusters. one cluster of fields was located near the Grand Island Post Office, and the other along the same road in a township located 15 to 20 miles to the northeast. Here, fields were among the largest in the study area, averaging 22 acres. Some very large fields with 200 acres to 300 acres held probably wild hay instead of planted crops. Pioneers found a ready market for wild hay at Fort Kearney, about 30 to 40 miles to the southwest. Considering the large size of fields and the flatness of the prairie, it is entirely possible that fields were reported more completely in the two portions of the Platte Valley than elsewhere. Accordingly, the Platte Valley may actually have contained a considerably smaller proportion of cropland than appears from the record. Furthermore, later dates of surveys could have contributed to larger fields in the Platte Valley. Perhaps, improved agricultural equipment was available for use on these later fields.

As reported, the outlying territory held only twelve fields of about average size, 15 acres. Here, five fields were clustered about a settlement of undefined character located near the confluence of Willow Creek with the Elkhorn River. Other fields were spaced widely: one at Bennett's Trading Post, one at the stage station near the eastern part of the outlying territory, and the other about six miles south of it.

Distribution of Extractive Features

Approximately one half of the compact settlements of eastern Nebraska were reported to have had steam saw mills (Figure 3, 4).[18] Along the Missouri Valley and its larger tributaries, groves of standing timber were relatively abundant, and here, saw mills were common features of early settlement. Most saw mills were erected either at nucleated settlements or within groves of timber standing within their hinterlands. The steam and water powered saw mills that were erected in the hinterlands of nucleated settlements were linked to them by wagon roads.

The map of extractive features (Figure 4) shows the distribution of saw mills that were built near standing timber within the hinterlnlds of nucleated settlements, and those that were erected at waterfalls along larger river valleys tributary to the Missouri. Most saw mills, whether near compact settlements or in groves of standing timber, were powered by steam engines. However, at least nine saw mills were powered by falling water. Below waterfall sites many saw mills were placed adjacent to mill ponds. The distribution of nine waterfall sites where saw mills were erected follow: Two water powered saw mills were placed on Weeping Water Creek. One saw mill was erected at a water fall on the north fork of Weeping Water Creek, and another was located at a fall on the south fork of it.[19] A short distance north of Nebraska City, a saw mill and its associated mill pond were placed on a small stream near its confluence with the Missouri River.[20] Southwest of Omaha City, a water powered saw mill was built at a falls on the south fork of the Big Papillion Creek.[21] About 12 miles south of Nebraska City, a saw mill and mill pond were constructed on Camp Creek near its confluence

---

18 Settlements with steam saw mills along the Missouri Valley included Niobrara, Ponca, St. Johns, Omadi, Tekama, Cuming, DeSoto, Ft. Calhoun, Florence, Omaha City, Bellevue, Nebraska City, South Nebraska City, Kearney City, Brownville, and Nemaha. Elsewhere, Columbus in the Platte Valley and Fontenelle in the Elkhorn Valley had steam saw mills.

19 U.S.L.S., *op. cit.*, T10N, R13E, June 24-July 3, 1856.

20 U.S.L.S., *op. cit.*, T9N, R13E, November 26-December 10, 1855.

21 U.S.L.S., *op. cit.*, T14N, R13E, June 7-14, 1856.

with the Missouri River.[22] West of Rock Bluffs a water powered saw mill was erected at the site of a falls on Rock Creek,[23] and about six miles to the south, another was place don a small creek near its confluence with the Missouri River.[24] About 15 miles southwest of Nebraska City, a saw mill was built at the falls of the Little Nemaha River.[25] Finally, another was erected north of Salem at the fall site of the north fork of the Big Nemaha River.[26] In addition to the water powered saw mills in the countryside, two steam powered saw mills were located in the southern Missouri Valley. One was placed at the platted townsite of La Platte, and the other was erected on Sonora Island, one mile north of Brownville in the Missouri River.[27]

Unlike the south Missouri Region, where nine water powered saw mills were erected, all seven saw mills in the countryside of the north Missouri Valley were powered by steam. They were placed in the vicinity of the following nucleated settlements: Niobrara, Logan, Central and Tekama (Figure 3). In some places one or two steam saw mills were erected within groves of standing timber. East of Tekama, two steam saw mills operated in the "Cross Timbers" grove on the floodplain along the Missouri River. Also, two steam saw mills operated near Logan: one at the "Logan Timber" to the northwest, and the other in timber to the north.

Except near the Missouri Valley and its larger tributaries, timber was scarce. Few saw mills were erected in such valleys as the Platte and Elkhorn. Two saw mills were recorded within the Platte Valley, a steam saw mill along the Wood River and a water powered saw mill at the paper town of Franklin. In the Elkhorn Valley, steam saw mills were built near Fontenelle and at Westpoint, a platted townsite. On a per capita basis, saw mills were almost as frequent here as along the Missouri Valley.

During 1856, coal and limestone were extracted along the Missouri Valley and some of its larger tributary valleys (Figure 4). A coal bank was being worked near Nemaha where it outcropped in the Little Nemaha

---

22 U.S.L.S., *op. cit.*, T7N, R14E, December 6-20, 1855.

23 U.S.L.S., *op. cit.*, T11N, R14E, April 5-May 8, 1856.

24 U.S.L.S., *op. cit.*, T10N, R13E, April 7-12, 1856.

25 U.S.L.S., *op. cit.*, T7N, R12E, November 15-26, 1856.

26 U.S.L.S., *op. cit.*, T1N, R15E, November 15, 1855-February 6, 1856.

27 U.S.L.S., *op. cit.*, T5N, R16E, January 24-31, 1856.

Valley.[28] Coal was mined to a limited extent in the southeastern extremity of the Missouri Valley.[29] Although other coal veins outcropped along large valleys of southeastern Nebraska, pioneers did not mine them at the time of original survey. However, prospects for this industry seemed good enough to some settlers for organization of at least one coal mining company. In December, 1857, the Otoe Coal Mining Company was incorporated at Nebraska City.[30]

Limestone quarries were more numerous than coal mines. Near Plattsmouth, limestone was quarried at several bluff sites, and lime of excellent quality was burned from this stone. A few limestone quarries were located among bluffs near Omaha City. Here, limestone was easily accessible and described as of excellent quality. The Weeping Water Valley had several limestone quarries.[31] In the middle reach of this valley, two quarries were being worked at the time of survey. Although other outcroppings of coal, limestone, and sandstone were recorded by surveyors, they were not actively mined at the time of original land survey.

Clay, sand, and gravel pits were worked at a few sites along the Missouri Valley. Near Omaha City, a stone quarry and a sand and gravel pit were both in operation:

> One thousand bushels of lime and any quantity of stone for building purposes for sale by the perch or load—also coarse sand suitable for plastering and gravel for cement. Stone quarry, one mile south of Omaha City.[32]

Clay pits were worked near cities and many large towns because bricks were manufactured and used for construction there. Brick kilns were in operation at Florence, Omaha City, and Nebraska City. Along bluffs of the Missouri River near St. James and Dakota, clay of several different colors was extracted for manufacture of bricks and pottery.[33]

---

28 U.S.L.S., *op. cit.*, T4N, R16E, July 29-August 7, 1856.
29 U.S.L.S., *op. cit.*, T1N, R18E, July 7-14, 1856.
30 *Bellevue Gazette*, December 24, 1857.
31 U.S.L.S., *op. cit.*, T10N, R12E, May 8-19, 1856.
32 *The Nebraskian*, January 9, 1856.
33 U.S.L.S., *op. cit.*, T32N, R2E, November 10-15, 1858.

Along Salt Creek, several springs produced valuable salt. In 1856, it was reported that, "Western enterprise can seize the salt trade, and it can export the article instead of importing it."[34] In 1857, a small vat for boiling of salt water was used to extract salt from the spring water. Surveyors said that specimens of salt were very pure.[35]

Although iron ore was discovered within eastern Nebraska, it was never present in quantities large enough for commercial mining. A surveyor recorded the presence of fragments of iron ore near Cuming City.[36] High grade ore with 50 per cent iron content was reported at Iron Bluffs.[37]

Samples From the Pattern of Settlement

In order to describe some details of the pioneering process, seven plats have been chosen to characterize the major patterns of settlement in eastern Nebraska Territory. Wherever surveyors rated the utility of the natural landscape, their judgments have been included. In and near the Missouri Valley, townships have been chosen to represent clustered and linear patterns of dispersed dwellings. These clusterings of dispersed dwellings are illustrated at townships that encompass Omaha City, Niobrara, and Nebraska City. Linear patterns of dispersed dwellings are illustrated in townships that encompass Muddy Creek and also parts of the Big and Little Papillion creeks. Along the emigrant wagon road through the Platte Valley, two plats are described to illustrate this long linear pattern of dwellings.

Surveyed between November 21 and December 5, 1855, T2N, R16E (Figure 11) was divided into triangular sections. The Half-Breed Tract occupied the northeast Triangle. Like all Indian reservations, it was outside the public domain.

---

34 *Nebraska Advertiser*, September 13, 1856.
35 U.S.L.S., *op. cit.*, T10N, R6E, October 17-22, 1857.
36 U.S.L.S., *op. cit.*, T19N, R11E, March 19-27, 1856.
37 *The Nebraskian*, July 23, 1856.

Figure 11

TOWNSHIP N° 2 NORTH RANGE N° 16 EAST OF 6th PRINCIPAL MERIDIAN

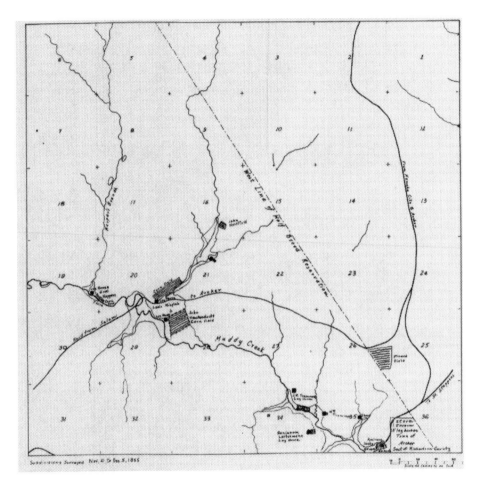

This plat is a direct tracing of the original, as are the plats that follow. On this plat the pattern of distribution of woods is emphasized by placing a line along the margin.

Settlement along Muddy Creek appears to be representative of that common throughout the prairie peninsula where pioneer settlement, while clinging to the woods, is indicated as beginning the occupation of the prairie.

All pioneer settlement was confined to the floodplain of Muddy Creek. It included the hamlet of Archer, which was the seat of Richardson County at the time of survey. Archer had one store, one tavern, and two log houses. Besides Archer, there were nine dispersed dwellings, identified as a house, and eight log houses. All settlement was located at the edge of groves of timber. Four different groves were spaced widely along Muddy Valley. Archer and five log farmhouses encircled a grove in the southeast part of Muddy Valley. In the west central part, two log houses were place on the edge of another grove. Farther upstream, settlers chose two smaller groves as sites for log houses. Two of the nine farmhouses were placed along wagon roads that led from Archer to Salem and Nemaha. Because wagon roads followed uplands instead of the Muddy Valley, many settlers were obliged to travel from their homes at least one half mile over the prairie before reaching a wagon road. Since this settled reach of Muddy Valley was situated 10 to 15 miles west of the Missouri River, these settlements were too far inland to import lumber here by team and wagon. Settlers at Archer and along Muddy Creek depended upon local groves of timber to build their log houses, to fence their fields, and to provide their firewood. Consequently, these early settlers built their log houses at the edge of the timber near Muddy Creek. Widespread settlement of upland prairie, where lumber was difficult to import, awaited the completion of settlement along edge-of-the-woods localities and the general willingness of pioneers to use sod for the construction of farmhouses.

Judging from their positions in relationship to Muddy Creek, in this township most fields appear to have been cultivated on well-drained terraces. Here, twelve fields were located; three were identified as cornfields and one as a plowed field. Totaling 142 acres, they varied in size from one half acre to 45 acres. The average size was about twelve acres. Where these fields were cultivated on benchland, the surveyor described the soil as very rich. As symbolized on the plat, three fields were fenced, two of them near Archer. Here, crops may have needed protection from livestock; or perhaps the settlers had just finished the job when the surveyors made the notation. Settlement in this township was distinctly rural. Archer served primarily as a trade center for farmsteads along Muddy Creek.

Surveyed January 1-29, 1856, T8N, R14E (Figure 12) includes the adjacent settlements of Nebraska City, South Nebraska City, and Kearney City. These settlements held 150 houses, 75 houses, and 50 houses respectively. Located in the north central part of the plat, they were located on bluffs of the Missouri Valley, where the river meandered across the northeast corner of the township. Three emigrant roads linked Nebraska City to major transportation places like Bennett's Ferry, Fort Kearney, and Marysville, Kansas. The surveyor described the natural landscape in this way:

> The quality of the land in this township is good rolling prairie and level bottom land. A little oak and hickory in groves is dispersed over the prairies. There is some good cottonwood in the bottom land in sections 13 and 24.

The groves that are mentioned in these notes are shown in Figure 12. This township has some good timber of construction quality; however, much of it was too small except for fencing or firewood.

Figure 12

TOWNSHIP N° 8 NORTH RANGE N° of 6ᵗʰ PRINCIPAL MERIDIAN

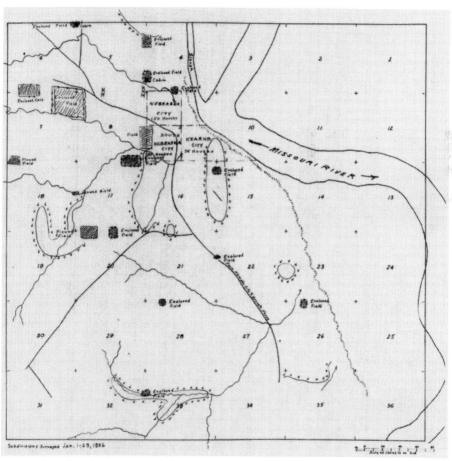

On this plat the pattern of distribution of woods is emphasized by Xs. Note the scarcity of houses in the countryside.

Here, the only dispersed dwellings were two cabins. One was placed about one fourth mile northwest of Nebraska City, and the other about one and one half miles to the northwest. The shortage of timber and the propensity of farmers for living in towns appear to have been limiting factors to spread of rural settlement onto the upland prairie. Although farmhouses were scarce, fields were abundant. Totaling 300 acres of cultivated land, the 17 fields ranged in size from 2 to 115 acres. The average field had about 18 acres. The six largest fields were placed on rolling uplands within two miles of Nebraska City. Although only about 10 per cent of fields were fenced in the area of study, fencing was a common practice near Nebraska City. Fences were built to protect crops from destruction by livestock. Here, almost three fourths of the fields were enclosed. To meet the heavy demand for lumber, these large urban settlements drew upon two sources. Lumber was not only imported by Missouri River steamboat, but it was also hauled over "wood roads", a term used by the surveyors, from nearby more wooded townships. Two saw mills were built in townships west of Nebraska City near timber from which lumber was hauled to Nebraska City.

Surveyed, June 10-14, 1856, T15N, R13E (Figure 13) included Omaha City and a cluster of farmhouses in its hinterland. With the additions of Pierce and the Omaha City Company, Omaha City incorporated almost three sections of upland that bordered the Missouri River. Omaha City is estimated to have had about 200 houses in 1856 when it was surveyed. West of the city, only seven farmhouses were shown, all distributed along wagon roads. However, 31 fields were located on rolling uplands in the central third of the township. Commonly of about 12 acres, they varied in size from 2 to 105 acres each. Despite the fact that crops were subject to damage by livestock that roamed freely, only two fields were shown as fenced. However, there was a long sod fence that surrounded three sides of about one and one half sections of prairie and timber land. This area, partially enclosed by sod fence, was located immediately west of Omaha City. It appears to have provided a partial barrier to the movement of livestock. Elsewhere on this plat, there were three other short sections of sod fence that were noted by the surveyor.

Much timber was needed in Omaha City, but timber was scarce in this township. The surveyors reported a few upland groves and some cottonwood on the bottomland. Little was available for fences or farmhouses. Of the 31 fields, only six fields had farmhouses accompanying them. Instead of living on upland prairie, it seems likely that most of these pioneer farmers lived in Omaha City, where lumber that was imported by steamboat was available for home building. In Omaha City, settlers found the basic necessities of shelter, fuel, and water. Five of the upland farmsteads had little or no timber, so these pioneers probably hauled in logs and firewood to their prairie farms from timber claims that were located a few2 miles away. Pioneers avoided settling the Missouri bottomland because it was subject to frequent overflow. As noted by a surveyor, upland soil where fields were cultivated was a good second rate clay loam.

Figure 13

TOWNSHIP N° 15 NORTH RANGE N° 13 EAST OF 6th PRINCIPAL MERIDIAN

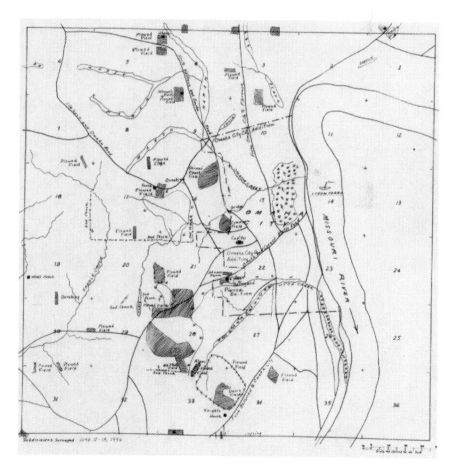

Surveyed June 12-30, 1856, T15N, R12E (Figure 14) was situated immediately west of the Omaha City township, and consequently, settlement here was located in its hinterland. The only timber was a few small groves of oak, elm, and walnut along the Big and Little Papillion creeks. The prairie was gently rolling except on the rich bottomland of the creeks, where four farmhouses were located. A house and two shanties were located in the Little Papillion Valley, and a cabin was built along the Big Papillion Creek. Another cabin was situated near the eastern edge of the township. Where a wagon road that crossed the center of the township intersected these two creeks, a shanty was located at one crossing and a cabin at the other. Other dwellings were placed one half mile or farther from the wagon road, none were laced more than one fourth mile from a creek. Probably, these pioneers had to haul timber for several miles to collect enough wood from the small scattered groves to build their cabins and to obtain firewood. Totaling about 80 acres, as designated on the plat, the 15 small breakings on floodplains ranged in size from two to 18 acres. None were fenced. As in the Omaha City township to the east, the abundance of unfenced fields in contrast to the scarcity of farmhouses resulted from absence of enough timber suitable for farmhouses and fences. Although it is possible that each farmer in the township tilled several fields, it seems more likely that farmers cultivated one breaking. Probably, most of these small breakings were tilled by farmers who reside din Omaha City and traveled back and forth to them.

Figure 14

TOWNSHIP N° 15 NORTH RANGE N° 12 EAST OF 6th PRINCIPAL MERIDIAN

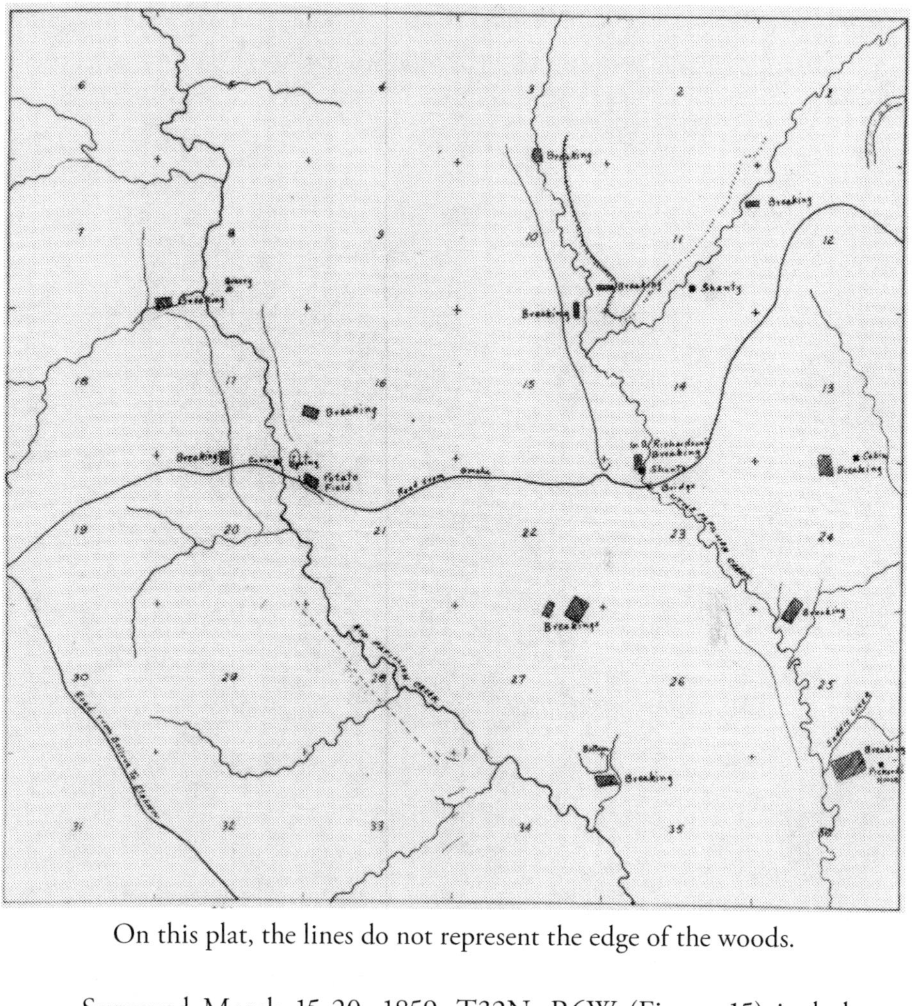

On this plat, the lines do not represent the edge of the woods.

Surveyed March 15-20, 1859, T32N, R6W (Figure 15) includes along its western margin, the Niobrara River and across the northern part, the Missouri River. Near the north central part, the village of Niobrara occupied a site on the right bank of the Missouri River. In 1856, Niobrara had a hotel, 15 to 20 houses, and a saw mill, according to the surveyor. This village had a steamboat landing that provided access to timbered islands of the Niobrara River. From them, logs could be transported by barge to the saw mill at Niobrara. The surveyors reported four dispersed dwellings in this township. One house and its plowed field were located west of the Niobrara River near the edge of the township. Two cabins were built south of Niobrara on the terrace of the Missouri River. These cabins and an adjoining field were located at the edge of the valley bluffs. From the wagon road that followed the bluffs of the Missouri and Niobrara rivers,

Figure 15

TOWNSHIP N° 32 NORTH RANGE N° 6 WEST OF 6ᵗʰ PRINCIPAL MERIDIAN

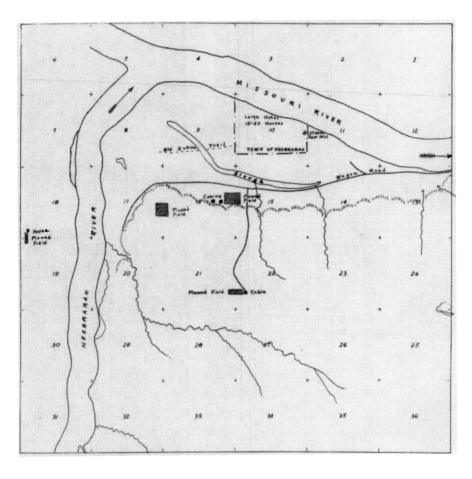

local roads led one mile north to Niobrara and one and one half miles southward to a third cabin and its adjoining plowed fields. A fourth field was tilled in an isolated locality about two miles southwest of Niobrara. These four fields included 85 acres of plowed land, and ranged in size from eight to 26 areas. Although three of the four fields were located near farmhouses, none of them were fenced. The surveyor rated the terrace soil as first class for cultivation. Considering the uplands as excessively broken, he rated them as second class for cultivation. Nevertheless, a pioneer farmer chose to build a cabin and cultivate his field on this upland. In fact, three of four fields were located on broken upland. These pioneer farmers preferred better drained field sites on uplands and on terrace land to the variably drained bottomland where inundation was likely.

Surveyed October 14-29, 1857, T17N, R6E (Figure 6) straddled the Platte Valley a few miles west of Fremont. Except for one dwelling near a right bank tributary of the Platte River and an Indian trail along the edge of the south bluff, the cultural features were distributed along the military road not far from the left bank of the Platte River. Here, the linear pattern of dispersed settlements included a platted townsite, Franklin, a log house, and five farmhouses. With a saw mill erected at the river's edge, the paper town of Franklin was laid out opposite a large heavily timbered island in the Platte River. In the Platte Valley, where timber was relatively sparse, timbered islands in the river became important locating factors both for platted

Figure 16

TOWNSHIP N° 17 NORTH RANGE N° 6 EAST OF 6ᵗʰ PRINCIPAL MERIDIAN

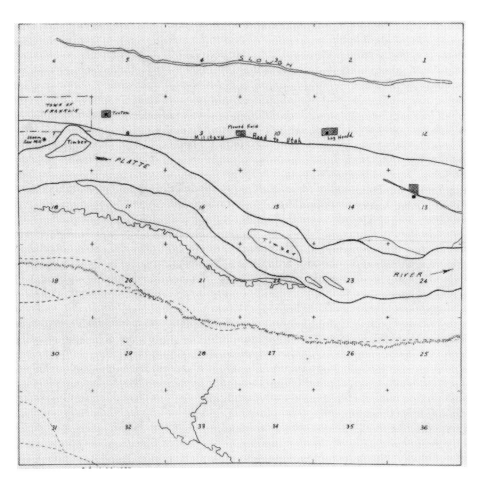

townsites and for actual nucleated settlements. The timber near the saw mill south of Franklin was mainly cottonwood, but there was some willow, elm, ash, and walnut in the township. Farmhouses and their accompanying fields were spaced from three fourths of a mile to two miles apart along the military wagon road. Totaling 33 acres, fields varied in size from four to 13 acres. The average field had only eight acres. Most of the fields and farmhouses were placed along the wagon road where it veered about one mile away from the river. These fields appear to have been located on well drained benchland, judging from their position on the plat, some distance from the river channel. The surveyor described the soil here as a sandy loam of first quality and well adapted to cultivation. Here, the pioneer economy was agricultural and emigrants provided an important segment of the local market.

Located in the Platte Valley about 30 to 35 miles southwest of Columbus, T13N, R6W (Figure 17) was surveyed October 19-29, 1862. Here, the Platte River traversed the township in a southwest to northeast direction. The surveyor commented that navigation of the Platte was impossible here because the water was shallow, and innumerable sand bars dotted the surface of the channel. Leading to Fort Kearney, emigrant roads followed both sides of the river. All dispersed settlements were placed along these emigrant roads.

Figure 17

TOWNSHIP Nº 13 NORTH RANGE Nº 6 WEST OF 6th PRINCIPAL MERIDIAN

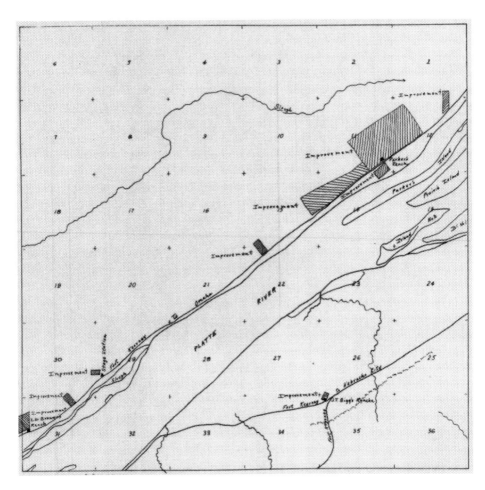

The surveyor said, "This township is being settled up rapidly along the banks of the Platte River. There are some good farms under cultivation in it." He regarded the terraces where settlement occurred, as first rate for cultivation. Except for one ranch and its 15 acre field south of the Platte, other settlements were located along the emigrant road that followed the left bank. Two ranches were spaced about six miles from one another, and a stage station was built near the ranch at the extreme southwest corner of the township. Totaling 480 acres, the eight fields ranged in size from four acres to 270 acres. Although most fields were only about 15 acres, the two largest fields included between 200 and 300 acres each. These were cultivated near the ranch close to the northeast corner of the township. None of the fields were fenced, a circumstance caused possibly by the scarcity of timber or omission of fences by surveyors. At these large fields, the rancher may have harvested wild hay to help overwinter his livestock and to sell to the emigrants for their livestock. It seems likely that ranches in this township were sustained mainly by trade with emigrants and perhaps by trade with Fort Kearney. The quartermaster purchased tons of hay from ranchers of the Platte Valley to feed the horses of their mounted troops.

Interpretation of the Distribution of Dispersed Settlement

The characteristics of the distribution of dispersed settlement that seem to warrant particular explanation are: (1) The relatively few farmhouses in eastern Nebraska compared to the number of houses in nucleated settlements, and the general lack of attention given by pioneers to the agricultural sector of the economy. (2) The concentration of most farmhouses and fields within less than 10 miles of nucleated river settlements along the Missouri Valley, from Florence southward. (3) The confinement of most remaining fields and farmhouses to the Platte Valley and to the middle and lower reaches of other large valleys in southeastern Nebraska. (4) The sparsity of fields and farmhouses along the northern Missouri Valley and in the outlying territory.

Generally, agriculture was a subordinate sector of the pioneer economy in eastern Nebraska during the early Territorial years, even after making allowance for under-representation of farm houses by the surveyors, as noted. This circumstance was revealed by relatively few farmhouses in the countryside compared with the large number of houses in cities, towns, and villages along the Missouri River (Figure 6). During early years of the Territorial period when the Missouri Valley was surveyed, agriculture was in its initial phase of development. Two or three years after the Missouri Valley had been surveyed, river cities and towns continued to import a considerable proportion of their food and other material needs. In 1859, for example, Omaha City's commerce was described as follows:

The steamboat, Florida, arrived from St. Louis. Omaha City was filled with white topped wagons, handcarts, and wheelbarrows. There were many reliable business houses. Steamers supplied dry goods, groceries, hardware, drugs, etc. Steamers leaving were loaded with cereals and esculents.[38]

Contemporary newspaper accounts recorded the introduction of farm machinery. Soon, farmers had more equipment than characterized many earlier settlements farther east. In June 1856, reaping and mowing machines were introduced for the first time.[39] By March 1857, at least two brands of reapers were available: McCormick's Patent Mower and Reaper, and Many's Patent Mower and Reaper.[40] Yet, some agricultural equipment, then in use, was very primitive by modern standards. For example, the following hand corn planter was advertised during June, 1856:

Wakefield's Hand Corn-Planter is used as a cane or walking stick – adjust it to plant at the desired depth and to drop any required number of seeds in a hill. Western Corn Planters Company. Office at 84 Main Street; St. Louis, Missouri.[41]

In Nebraska Territory, primitive equipment like this hand cornplanter was undoubtedly among the factors that limited early corn fields to a small size. Regardless of the vast potentialities for agriculture within eastern Nebraska, the agricultural sector of the early Territorial economy assumed a subordinate role. Urban pursuits predominated. The Territorial census of 1860 shows that only 4,437 pioneers (38 per cent) of the 11,581 persons engaged in occupations were employed as farmers and farm laborers. The outfitting of emigrants and of local farmers involved settlers in a variety of commercial and manufacturing activities. Transportation related activities employed many teamsters

38 Andreas, *op. cit.*,. p. 699.
39 *The Nebraskian*, June 11, 1856.
40 *Nebraska News*, March 21, 1857.
41 *Nebraska Advertiser*, June 7, 1856.

and hotel keepers. Furthermore, construction and speculation on town property engaged many laborers and promoters at river towns.

On the other hand, the most important of the natural resources in eastern Nebraska, the soil, although recognized by surveyors as potentially productive for expanded agriculture, was largely unutilized by the young, but growing, Territorial settlement. Consequently, the financial crash of 1857 was especially hard on the Territorial economy:

The financial crash swallowed all the money in the country and scarcity was felt in the Territory because nearly everything that was consumed was brought from the States, as very little had as yet been produced from the soil.[42]

After the panic of 1857, little impetus was given to the widespread rural settlement and agricultural development of eastern Nebraska until 1859. The change in destination of Nebraska produce from the home market to the St. Louis market is described by Graebner, as follows:

Produce offered for sale in 1858 was still so limited and demands created by freighters and emigrants so extensive that grain and livestock markets were almost entirely local. But commission merchants from St. Louis appeared in Nebraska that summer, offering a wider market for corn, and the *Omaha Times* reported shipments of potatoes, corn, and oats down the river during autumn months of 1858. Finally, in 1859, the heavy movement of grain by wagon into the river communities broke the home market completely.[43]

From Florence southward along the Missouri Valley, most farmhouses and fields were clustered within less than 10 miles of compact settlements along the river (Figure 6). Here, as in the territory generally, the majority of settlers were engaged in urban pursuits. Agriculture was carried on primarily to supply the river settlements. Some food crops and feed grains were exported to St. Louis, although as noted previously,

---

42 Andreas, *op. cit.*, p. 1127.
43 Graebner, Norman A., "Nebraska's Missouri River Frontier, 1854-1860", *Nebraska History*, Volume 42, Number 4, December, 1961, pp. 229-30.

Nebraska pioneers imported other groceries to meet some of their food requirements.

The numbers of farmhouses in the vicinity of compact river settlements were not in proportion to their sizes. That is, farmhouses were often as common near hamlets as in the vicinity of cities and large towns. It appears that rates of growth of cities and large towns exceeded rates of rural settlement in their hinterlands. The size of river settlements corresponded more closely to the number of fields in their hinterlands than to the number of farmhouses there (Figure 6). This closer correspondence between size of urban settlements and number of fields is attributed to the observation that some fields were isolated from farmhouses and others were tilled beside them. According to the following report of 1856, many farmers lived in river towns of the Missouri Valley:

All towns on the western side of the Missouri River flourish and are built more rapidly than on the eastern bank, and for the reason that all produce raised west of the river must find its way to the river for shipment. The Swiss system of farmers living in towns instead of being isolated on their farms exists. This causes more sociability, and accounts for the number and beauty of western towns and villages.[44]

This system of farmers living in river towns accounts for many of the fields that were clustered in the vicinity of Missouri River urban settlements and tilled along wagon roads there. Consequently, the total fields clustered in the hinterlands of river towns include those tilled by urban residents and those tilled by rural residents whose farmhouses and fields were placed together on the same claim.

West of the Missouri Valley, most fields and farmhouses were confined to the Platte Valley and to the middle and lower reaches of large valleys to the south. Here, settlement was about three fourths dispersed, and the pioneers were mainly farmers. They settled on claims of 160 acres, as explained by the following newspaper entry:

Rights of Pre-emption The Act of 4th September, 1841, declares that 160 acres are all that one person can pre-empt. Thus it seems that 160

---

44 *The Nebraskian*, August 13, 1856.

acres is the only sized parcel to be obtained by pre-emption *before* the day of land sales.[45]

Imported goods from St. Louis were less accessible because travel was slow between these tributary valleys and the Missouri River. Consequently, economic opportunities other than farming were limited, so, except for a few small settlements that were largely centers of rural service and trade, settlement beyond the Missouri Valley was dispersed, not nucleated.

The Platte Valley was settled mainly by farmers along the wagon route that followed the left bank of the Platte River. Here, they were able to market their agricultural commodities to passing emigrants instead of having to transport commodities for distances as far as 125 miles to towns along the Missouri River. The route of the Platte was desirable for pioneer farmers and emigrants because it provided the natural resources that were essential for them. The three citations that follow reveal judgments of the surveyors concerning the suitability of the route of the Platte for rural settlement. They assessed the availability of essential natural resources like water, grass, timber, and soil. Township 15N, R4W, situated about 25 miles southwest of Columbus, was described thus:

The Platt River is a large stream, averaging more than one mile wide with water in many channels amid numerous sand bars . . . . Its banks are low with grass growing to the water's edge in many places, but without indication of inundation . . . . It furnishes cool and potable water to emigrant (and pioneer) both for himself and his stock.[46]

Township 13N, R6W was located about 20 miles northeast of the Grand Island Post Office. Here, the surveyor said:

This township is being settled up rapidly along the banks of the Platte River. There are now some good farms under cultivation in it.

---

45 *Nebraska Advertiser*, December 13, 1856.
46 U.S.L.S., *op. cit.*, T15N, R4W, September 20-27, 1862.

Timber – It contains some very good timber, principally cottonwood and cedar on some islands and in clumps along the banks of the river.[47]

In the case of Township 12N, R8W, situated immediately northeast of Grand Island, The surveyor emphasized the quality of the land for agriculture as follows:

The quality of the land is very good and well adapted to farming. It is high rich and level bottom . . . . The southeast corner borders on the Platte River which stream furnishes sufficient water for all purposes . . . . There are now several persons living in the township.[48]

The farmers of the Platte Valley grew a variety of crops, but mainly wild hay and corn because these crops were in great demand by settlers and emigrants for livestock feed. The township encompassing the Platte and Shell valleys for 25 miles east of Columbus, Platte County, in 1857, was reported to have had "551 acres of prairie broken – 169 were planted to corn, 14 to potatoes, 1 to beans, and 1/2 an acre to turnips. Five hundred and thirteen tons of hay were cut and put up."[49] At a yield of one ton per acre, there may have been about as large an acreage cut for hay as all the land that was broken. In this county, the farmers found a ready market for their surplus production with the emigrants who streamed through the Platte Valley. Completion of the Union Pacific Railroad in 1864 stimulated further agricultural settlement of the Platte Valley because Eastern markets were tapped for the first time. A decade ahead of the Platte Valley, the year 1855 was noted by Poggi as the close of steamboat preeminence in the trade of the Illinois Valley and the beginning of railroad supremacy there.[50] Other than the Platte and Missouri, the middle and lower reaches of valleys in southeastern Nebraska held most of the remaining fields and farmhouses. The records of the survey and, in 1857, this report of the governor of Nebraska Territory revealed that many pioneer farmers

47 U.S.L.S., *op. cit.*, T13N, R6W, October 19-29, 1862.
48 U.S.L.S., *op. cit.*, T 12N, R8W, August 11-16, 1866.
49 *Bellevue Gazette*, December 3, 1857.
50 Poggi, Edity M., *The Prairie Province of Illinois*, University of Illinois, 1934, pp. 102-103.

preferred to build their farmhouses and to cultivate their fields on the rich terraces and bottomland of the river valleys:

The rich bottom and bench lands of the Missouri and Platte valleys and their numerous tributary valleys, and the small tributaries along the route of the Platte are fast filling up with settlers who are already realizing promising returns from their labors.[51]

The middle and lower reaches of the following large river valleys were occupied by fields or farmhouses: Papillion, Weeping Water, Little Nemaha, Muddy, and Big Nemaha. Here, the farmers built their farmhouses and usually cultivated their fields on terraces, or, in the case of the Papillion, the floodplain, and in some places on adjacent uplands. These relatively large valleys held a few hamlets. They served as trade and service centers for rural settlers. Unlike the Platte Valley, these valleys did not receive a flow of emigrants to provide farmers with a convenient market for their field crops. Consequently, the features of settlement, whether mainly fields or farmhouses or a combination of both, varied from valley to valley. For example, in the Papillion Valley, isolated fields were the most common features. Here, Omaha City was near enough to provide a convenient market for pioneer farmers, and perhaps, some farmers commuted back and forth between their fields and Omaha City. The scarcity of farmhouses is attributed primarily to sparcity of construction timber along the Papillion Valley, and secondarily, to preference of many farmers for urban living or because of delays in constructing houses. Along Muddy Creek Valley, log farmhouses and fields were arranged in pairs on each claim. Here, the hamlet of Archer provided a convenient place for farmers to market their crops and to purchase their supplies.

In the Big and Little Nemaha valleys, log farmhouses were built along remote reaches where fields were not recorded by surveyors. In view of the great under-representation of fields in section interiors, however, it seems safe to assume that there were at least some fields present in this area. Nevertheless, settled reaches of these valleys were situated so far west of the Missouri River that these pioneers may have specialized in raising livestock, which could be driven to market,

---

51 *Nebraska News*, December 19, 1857.

rather than producing grain that would have been more cumbersome to transport to market. Both of these valleys had scattered groves of timber at the edge of which pioneers built their log houses. South of the Big Nemaha Valley, Indians of the Sac and Fox Reservation tilled a few isolated corn fields.

Along the northern Missouri Valley, twelve small compact settlements included about 20 per cent of all houses that were recorded by surveyors and estimated from the 1860 census of population for the area of study. On the other hand, this subregion held only 7 per cent of the fields and 7 per cent of the farmhouses that were recorded in the area of study by surveyors. Only a few fields and farmhouses were clustered in the vicinity of six of the twelve hamlets, villages, and small towns that were commonly spaced widely along the valley. Fields and farmhouses were sparse either because the markets for agricultural commodities were limited or possibly because surveyors missed a lot of them on the rolling land. Except for Dakota, the other eleven small compact settlements of the northern Missouri Valley were not involved in emigrant outfitting. The surveyors' notes revealed that most settlements here did not have the necessary variety of business facilities for outfitting, and that most of them did not have ferry crossings. Many of the emigrants who crossed the Missouri River at Dakota traveled southward to Florence or Omaha City in order to outfit themselves before heading westward through the Platte Valley. Since they took on produce and other food at these outfitting centers, they needed few agricultural commodities while en route along the northern Missouri Valley. Generally, sparseness of dispersed settlement is attributed to these circumstances: small markets at hamlets, villages, and small towns; food imports from St. Louis; and, conservative requirements by emigrants for agricultural commodities.

Three groups of farmers who came to eastern Nebraska from Germany and Ireland were adventurous inasmuch as they opted to settle along the Missouri and Platte rivers near their western fringes of settlement. Perhaps they preferred fringe sites that offered some degree of isolation from other settlers. In the northwestern extremity of the Missouri Valley, during 1858, the survey described the farm dwellings of German settlers and included an explanation for the scarcity of their fields:

A settlement has been made in sections 8, 16, and 17 by a party of Germans, but little improvement has yet been made except in the erection of cabins . . . . A field of about 30 acres in the SW 1/4 of section 17 is the principal agricultural improvement in the township.[52]

In the Western part of the Platte Valley, 12 farmhouses were closely spaced along the wagon road near the Grand Island Post Office. During 1866, the settlers and the township were described as follows:

It has considerable cottonwood timber along the north channel, and is every way well adapted to agricultural purposes, and is already quite well settled with a thriving German settlement . . . . There are more settlements in this township than any other. The settlers are Germans who devote their time to farming. The soil brings forth crops of all kinds.[53]

In June, 1861, nine houses were closely spaced along Shell Creek, a left bank tributary of the Platte River, located north of Columbus. Judging from names mentioned by the surveyors: Carrick, Gleeson, Kelly, and Darreen, these farmers claimed Ireland as their native land. The German states and Ireland were the major foreign countries of origin for settlers of Nebraska Territory, at least as recorded within the Territorial census of 1860.

In the outlying territory, there was very little settlement because several factors inhibited it during the Territorial period. Probably the most basic problem was related to remoteness of the outlying territory from Missouri River towns. Here, long distances of travel coupled with slow means of transportation were retarding factors for settlement. By team and wagon, settlers did not travel ordinarily more than 20 miles per day, and even the most remotely located farmhouses were no further than 60 miles west of the Missouri River. Moreover, the cost of importing manufactured goods from Missouri River towns by team and wagon would have been restrictive, if not prohibitive. There was a scarcity of wagon roads and bridges, and a lack of farm access roads. Many rural settlers, perhaps the majority, had to travel cross-country

52 U.S.L.S., *op. cit.*, T33N, R2W, September 4-8, 1858.
53 U.S.L.S., *op. cit.*, T11N, R9W, August 6-10, 1866.

for part of the way between their farms and the wagon roads leading to river towns. The plight of back country settlers was expressed succinctly in June, 1856, by the following statement:

The settler here has no access to his home nor outlet to the markets abroad, but such as the slow, cumbersome, and expensive facilities that his team and wagon afford him. While such is the case, the interior must settle slowly. The emigrant will be loath to seek a home distant from the river, if in so doing, he isolates himself from the world abroad and is shut out from all intercourse with his fellow men, save, only those who chance to have settled immediately around him.[54]

Above the Platte Valley, the outlying territory was north of the cutoff routes from the Missouri River to Fort Kearney, so that even the few stage stations and trading posts that occurred elsewhere were absent here. Moreover, distance to markets was a factor that inhibited settlement. Except along the Platte Valley, therefore, settlement rarely occurred farther than 15 miles from the Missouri River. North of the Platte Valley, the outlying territory had few large valleys that could accommodate settlement. Here, the Niobrara and Elkhorn valleys were large, but they attracted only a few farmhouses. Elsewhere on rolling uplands and along small headward valleys of the back country, there was not enough timber (Figure 3) nor enough surface water,[55] except for some intermittent flow, to support settlement. Furthermore, ground water was too deep to be reached by well digging.[56] Inadequate supplies of timber and unreliable sources of surface water from intermittent streams were limiting factors in early settlement of the outlying territory. Therefore, the settlement of localities where one or more of the essential natural resources were not readily available was delayed until the advent of new technology permitted settlement after the Territorial period.

In the outlying territory, reasons for lack of settlement south of the Platte Valley were similar to those north of it. For example, upper reaches of the large tributaries, small tributaries, and rolling uplands lacked settlers because timber of building quality and perennially

---

54 *Nebraska Advertiser*, June 21, 1856.
55 U.S.D.I., *Geological Survey, State of Nebraska*, Edition of 1921.
56 U.S.D.A., *Soil Survey*, Cass County, Nebraska, March 1941, p. 4.

flowing surface water were absent. Small streams were intermittent, and depth to ground water was too great for hand dug wells, the method commonly employed by early settlers. South of the Platte, moreover, much of the outlying territory was farther west of the Missouri River, and team and wagon travel was just as slow and cumbersome as north of the Platte. However, here, the cutoff wagon routes between the Missouri River and Fort Kearney crossed the outlying territory. They provided short cuts for emigrants and stagecoaches to Fort Kearney from Kansas, Nebraska City, and Plattsmouth. Nevertheless, these cutoff routes attracted few settlers except at a few stream crossing where timber and surface water were sufficient for occasional express stations (Figure 6). At these crossings, stage stations, the usual features of settlement, were widely spaced because they performed services that were needed infrequently along the overland routes. A few widely spaced trading posts with competitive functions also occurred here. Settlers did not occupy the area east of the Salt-Platte confluence because the Pawnee Indians held this part of the public domain. Settlement of this valuable timber and farming land awaited removal of the Pawnee to the site of a new reservation in the vicinity of the Loup River.

The westward advance of rural settlement beyond the Missouri Valley was encouraged by the opportunity for settlers to claim land at government prices. The availability of a great deal of land for pre-emption within the public domain was a tremendous incentive for the rural settlement of Nebraska Territory. Furthermore, settlers were concerned, in 1856, with delaying the sale of land until they had time to open up their farms:

We are opposed to appropriations, or meddling, in any way with the Public Lands, at present, other than making such arrangements that the actual settlers can pre-empt, and pay for their land at $1.25 per acre, along at such times as they are able. We are satisfied that great injury would result from bringing the Public Lands to sale, short of two years hence, at least. Give the settlers time to open up their farms, get things comfortable around them, and then pay for their land.[57]

---

57 *Nebraska Advertiser*, June 21, 1856.

The cost of land pre-empted within the public domain was far below the cost of improved land on farms. Near Nebraska City in 1856, for example, the average price of improved land, fenced and under cultivation, was $8.25 per acre.[58] This price was six times greater than the cost of land offered by the government for pre-emption.

The profitableness of growing crops and raising livestock was an incentive for the pre-emption of claims on the western fringe of settlement. On many claims, 10 to 20 acres of land were broken and planted to corn. Many pioneer farmers were able to pay for a 160 acre claim in a single season. Near Nebraska City in 1856, for example, the average yield of corn was 75 bushels and the price 25 cents per bushel. Consequently, profit from a corn field having 20 acres or more was enough to pay for a 160 acre pre-emption in one season.[59] Rural citizens protected their claims from intruders by organizing societies for that purpose. Commonly, protective societies were organized among the farmers of a township or a county. For example, the citizens of T6N, R15E met in a shop on Honey Creek during July, 1856, to draft the rules for protection of their claims. They agreed to publish the proceedings of subsequent meetings in the *Nebraska Advertiser*.[60]

Livestock represented a considerable source of wealth to pioneer farmers because they were inexpensive to fatten on hay and prairie grasses. In 1856, for example, hay was only $1.00 per ton. In winter, it provided a substantial part of the feed for livestock. During the summer, livestock were pastured exclusively on the lush prairie. The excellent quality of the prairie near Brownville was described as follows in 1856: "Here our cattle roam at large, and become fat and sleek upon the prairie grass and wild pea, abounding in this region. Butter has excellent flavor".[61] Although feed was free or inexpensive in the form of prairie or hay, livestock commanded handsome prices when compared with prices of other agricultural products. The average cost of a team of horses was $250.00, and a yoke of oxen brought $90.00. Cattle were somewhat less expensive. Milk cows cost from $20.00 to $40.00 per head, and common cattle about $15.00 apiece.[62] Because livestock

58 *Nebraska Advertiser*, August 30, 1856.
59 *Ibid.*
60 *Nebraska Advertiser*, August 23, 1856.
61 *Nebraska Advertiser*, January 7, 1856.
62 *Nebraska Advertiser*, August 30, 1856.

roamed at large over the prairie, many were lost; and because of their value, their owners sought to reclaim them by publishing estray notices in the Territorial newspapers.[63] Public pressure was brought to bear on the problem. In January, 1856, the Territorial legislature passed an act that required farmers to restrain their swine and sheep from running at large.[64] Bogue has described pioneer methods used to restrain livestock in the prairie peninsula farther east where timber was in short supply:

When he sought to fence his crops against marauding livestock, the prairie farmer faced the timber problem at its most acute period. Farmers suggested a variety of substitutes for rail fences . . . . By the 1850's osage orange had emerged from a host of competing hedge plants as a practicable living hedge . . . . Meanwhile many prairie farmers had supported an institutional solution to the fencing problem. This was the herd law, which held owners of livestock responsible for their confinement.[65]

63 *Nebraska Advertiser*, December 20, 1856.
64 *The Nebraskian*, January 30, 1856.
65 Bogue, Allan G., "Farming in the Prairie Peninsula, 1830-1890," *The Journal of Economic History*, Vol. XXIII, No. 1, March 1963, pp. 6-7.

BIBLIOGRAPHY

Articles

Barrows, Harlan H. "The Geography of the Middle Illinois Valley," *Bulletin No. 15 Illinois State Geological Survey*, 1910, (reviewed *Bulletin American Geographical Society* 1910, Vol. 42, No. 680-682).

Bogue, Allan G. "Farming in the Prairie Peninsula, 1830-1890," *The Journal of Economic History*, Vol. 23, No. 1, March, 1963, p. 3-29.

Dale, Edward E. "Wood and Water: Twin Problems of the Prairie Plains," *Nebraska History*, Vol. 29, No. 2, June, 1948, pp. 87-104.

Graebner, Norman A. "Nebraska Missouri River Frontier, 1854-1860," *Nebraska History*, Vol. 42, No. 4, December, 1961, pp. 213-236.

Guide to the Union Pacific Railroad Lands. Union Pacific Railroad Company. Omaha, Nebraska, 1870.

Hewes, Leslie. "Some Features of Early Woodland and Prairie Settlement in a Central Iowa County," *Annals of the Association of American Geographers*, Vol. XL, March, 1950, No. 1.

Jordan, Terry G. "Between the Forest and the Prairie," *Agricultural History*, Vol. 38, No. 4, October, 1964, pp. 205-216.

Pattison, William D. "A Partial Answer to the Question, Who Has Exploited the Public Land Survey Plats and Field Notes for Their Descriptive Content?" *Annals of the Association of American Geographers*, September, 1955, p. 289.

Poggi, Edith Muriel. "The Prairie Province of Illinois," *Illinois Studies in Social Science*, Vol. XIX, No. 3, 1934, pp. 97-120. Published as University of Illinois Bulletin, Vol. XXXI, No. 42, 1934.

Pool, R. J., Weaver, J. E., and Jean, F. C. "Further Studies in the Ecotone between Prairie and Woodland," *University of Nebraska Studies*, Vol. XVIII, pp. 1-47, figs, 1918.

Schafer, Joseph K. "Partial Presentation of Early Settlement in Wisconsin in 23 Selected Townships," *Wisconsin Domesday Book Town Studies*, Vol. I, Madison: State Historical Society of Wisconsin, 1924.

Vance, James E. "The Oregon Trail and Union Pacific Railroad: A Contrast in Purpose," *Annals of the Association of American Geographers*, December, 1961, p. 365.

Whittlesey, Derwent. "Early Geography in Northern Illinois," *Science*, Vol. 81, 1935, pp. 227-229.

Books

Andreas, A. T. *History of the State of Nebraska*. Chicago: The Western Historical Company, 1882.

Bogue, Margaret Beattie. *Patterns from the Sod*, Land Use and Tenure in the Grand Prairie, 1850-1900. Springfield: Illinois State Historical Library, 1959.

Brown, Ralph H. *Historical Geography of the United States*, Harcourt Brace and Co., New York, 1948.

Brunhes, Jean. *Human Geography*. New York: Rand McNally and Co., 1920.

James, Preston E., and Jones, Clarence F. *American Geography: Inventory and Prospect*. Syracuse University Press, 1954.

Olson, James. *History of Nebraska*. University of Nebraska Press, 1955.

Pound, R., and Clements, F. E. *Phyto-Geography of Nebraska*. University of Nebraska, 1900.

Sale, Randall D., and Karn, Edwin D. *American Expansion: A Book of Maps*, Dorsey Series in American History, Dorsey Press Inc., Homewood, Illinois, 1962.

Sauer, Carl Ortwin. *The Morphology of Landscape*. University of California, Publications in Geography, Vol. 2, No. 2, Berkeley: University of California Press, 1925.

Weaver, John E. *North American Prairie*. Lincoln, Nebraska: Johnsen Publishing Co., 1954.

Interviews

Statements by Willis L. Brown, State Surveyor. Personal interviews. Lincoln, Nebraska, 1963.

Maps

Gast, Leopold, and Brother, lithographers. Corondel Avenue, St. Louis, Missouri. *The Territory of Nebraska, Embracing the Public Survey up to the Summer of 1857*. Scale: 5 miles to 1 inch. (Compiled and drawn in the Surveyor General's Office from Original Notes by Quin, Smith and Van Zandt).

Map Publishing Office. 65 Chestnut Street, St. Louis, Missouri. *A New Map of the Principal Routes to the Gold Region of Colorado Territory*, 1862.

U.S. Department of Agriculture. *Soil Map. Nebraska. Dakota County Sheet*, 1919. Scale: 1:62,500. Lincoln, Nebraska.

U.S. Department of Agriculture. *Soil Map. Nebraska. Douglas County Sheet*, 1919. Scale: 1:62,500. Lincoln, Nebraska.

U.S. Department of Agriculture. *Soil Map. Nebraska. Nemaha County Sheet*, 1919. Scale: 1:62,500. Lincoln, Nebraska.

U.S. Department of Agriculture. *Soil Map. Nebraska. Washington County Sheet*, 1919. Scale: 1:62,500. Lincoln, Nebraska.

U.S. Department of Agriculture. Nebraska Soil Survey. *Soil Map of Richardson County*, 1915. Scale: 1:62,500. Lincoln, Nebraska.

U.S. Department of Interior, Geological Survey. *State of Nebraska*, 1921. Scale: 1:500,000.

U.S. Department of Interior, Geological Survey. *Nebraska-Iowa-Missouri, Nebraska City Quadrangle*. Washington, D.C. Surveyed in 1905. Scale: 1:62,500.

U.S. Department of Interior, Geological Survey. *Nebraska-Iowa, Nehawka Quadrangle*. Washington, D.C. Surveyed in 1934-1935. Scale: 1:62,500.

U.S. Department of Interior, Geological Survey. *Nebraska, Weeping Water Quadrangle*. Edition of 1903, reprinted in 1949. Scale: 1:125,000. Washington, D.C.

University of Nebraska, Conservation and Survey Division. *Nebraska, Reconnaissance Soil Conservation Survey Showing Generalized Classes of Land According to Use Capability*. Lincoln, Nebraska, 1942. Scale: 1:600,000.

University of Nebraska, Conservation and Survey Division. *Topographic Regions Map of Nebraska*, 1963.

Newspapers

Bellevue Gazette. Bellevue, Nebraska, 1856-1857.

Dakota City Herald. Dakota City, Nebraska, 1859.

DeSoto Pilot. DeSoto, Nebraska, 1857.

Huntsman's Echo, The. Wood River Center, Nebraska, 1860.

Nebraska Advertiser. Brownville, Nebraska, 1855-1857.

Nebraska News. Nebraska City, Nebraska, 1857.

Nebraskian. Omaha City, Nebraska, 1856.

Public Documents

General Land Office. *To the Surveyors General of Public Lands of the United States for the Surveying Districts Established in and since the Year 1850.* Government Printing Office, February 22, 1855.

U.S. Bureau of Census. *Statistical Atlas of the United States.* Prepared for the census of 1870.

U.S. Department of Agriculture, Bureau of Plant Industry. *Soil Survey. Cass County, Nebraska.* Series 1936, No. 5, March, 1941.

U.S. Department of Agriculture, Bureau of Chemistry & Soils. *Soil Survey of Knox County, Nebraska.* Series 1930, No. 25, 1930.

U.S. Department of Agriculture, Agricultural Research Administration, Bureau of Plant Industry, Soils, and Agricultural Engineering. *Soil Survey. Otoe County, Nebraska.* Series 1940, No. 6, August, 1950.

U.S. Department of Agriculture, Bureau of Chemistry and Soils. *Soil Survey. Platte County, Nebraska*. Washington: U.S. Government Printing Office, 1929.

U.S. Department of Agriculture. *Soil Survey of Sarpy County, Nebraska*. Washington, D.C., October, 1939.

U.S. Department of Agriculture, Weather Bureau. *Climatic Summary of the United States, Eastern Nebraska*, Section 39. Washington: Government Printing Office, 1932.

U.S. Government *Census*. Territory of Nebraska, 1860.

U.S. Land Survey. *Field Notes and Plats, Nebraska Territory*, 1854-1866.

University of Nebraska, Conservation and Survey Division. Nebraska Geological Survey. *Correlation of the Pleistocene Deposits of Nebraska*, Bulletin 15A. Lincoln, Nebraska, 1950.

University of Nebraska, Conservation and Survey Division. *Nebraska Soils*, Lincoln, Nebraska, 1959.

Published Dissertations

McManis, Douglas R. *The Initial Evaluation and Utilization of the Illinois Prairies, 1814-1840*. Research Paper No. 94. Chicago: The University of Chicago, Department of Geography, 1964.

Pooley, William V. "The Settlement of Illinois from 1830-1850," *University of Wisconsin Bulletin*, Historical Series, Vol. I, No. 4, Madison, 1908.

Unpublished Material

Barnes, Mary. "A History of Brownville, Nebraska." Unpublished Master's Thesis, University of Nebraska, 1933.

Burrill, Helen A. "A Geographic Interpretation of the Location and Development of Fremont, Nebraska." Unpublished Master's Thesis, University of Nebraska, 1927.

Caldwell, Harry H. "Plattsmouth, Nebraska: A Study in Urban Geography." Unpublished Master's Thesis, University of Nebraska, 1946.

Clayburn, Ansel. "Geographic Influences in the Development of Omaha, Nebraska." Unpublished Master's Thesis, University of Nebraska, 1927.

Danker, Donald Floyd. "Some Social Beginnings in Territorial Nebraska." Unpublished Ph.D. dissertation, University of Nebraska, 1955.

Garrett, Hubert. "A History of Brownville, Nebraska." Unpublished Master's Thesis, University of Nebraska, 1927.

Holtz, Milton S. "Early Settlement in Nebraska: A Study of Cass County, Nebraska." Unpublished Master's Thesis, University of Nebraska, 1964.

Jakl, Mary Ann. "The Immigration and Population of Nebraska to 1870." Unpublished Master's Thesis, University of Nebraska, 1936.

Jelen, Josephine. "Towns and Townsites in Territorial Nebraska." Unpublished Master's Thesis, University of Nebraska, 1934.

Mears, Louise W. "Some Geographical Influences in the Development of Southeastern Nebraska; Nemaha County in Particular." Unpublished Master's Thesis, University of Nebraska, 1912.

Melvin, Earl Ellsworth. "The Geographic Factors Operative in the Development of Hall County, Nebraska." Unpublished Master's Thesis, University of Nebraska, 1926.

Sellin, Lloyd Bernard. "Settlement of Nebraska to 1880." Unpublished Ph.D. Dissertation, University of Southern California, 1940.